THE BOY WHO NEVER GAVE UP

A Refugee's Epic Journey to Triumph

DR EMMANUEL TABAN

WITH ANDREW CROFTS

JONATHAN BALL PUBLISHERS

JOHANNESBURG · CAPE TOWN · LONDON

First published in South Africa in 2021 by
JONATHAN BALL PUBLISHERS
A division of Media24 (Pty) Ltd
PO Box 33977
Jeppestown
2043

This paperback edition published in 2022
Reprinted in 2022, 2023

ISBN 978-1-77619-196-3
ebook ISBN 978-1-77619-127-7

Every effort has been made to trace the copyright holders and to obtain their permission for the use of copyright material. The publishers apologise for any errors or omissions and would be grateful to be notified of any corrections that should be incorporated in future editions of this book.

www.jonathanball.co.za
www.twitter.com/JonathanBallPub
www.facebook.com/JonathanBallPublishers

Cover by Sean Robertson
Design and typesetting by Martine Barker
Set in Parisine and Baskerville
Printed and bound by Pinetown Printers

CONTENTS

LIST OF MAPS

PROLOGUE

'I will kill you like George Floyd!'

A droplet of spit fell on my cheek and I could smell the breath of the Tshwane Metro Police officer. His angry eyes bored into mine.

Seconds earlier, he and his partner had shoved first my wife, Motheo, and then me into their police van. It was a clear act of intimidation. They had pulled us over after I had crossed a solid white line while overtaking another vehicle. I don't normally dis-obey traffic rules but I was in a great hurry to get to Midstream Mediclinic in Centurion, where one of my COVID-19 patients was in the intensive care unit (ICU).

'Where's your phone?' he shouted. Another droplet of spit.

'It's in my car,' I lied. I had secretly slid it over to Motheo, whis-pering to her to send to a friend the photos and videos I'd taken of the vehicle registration number and the cops' faces. But they were all over us and she was too shaken to do anything. I saw her lip was still bleeding from when the traffic cop had wrestled her to the ground and into their van.

'Where's the phone? I saw it on you!'

The officer got into the van and started to search my body, but to no avail. 'I *will* kill you!' The next moment he grabbed me by the throat and started to throttle me.

Motheo is South African and I am South Sudanese. My particular shade of blackness and the fact that I do not speak Sepedi had fuelled the officers' antagonism. One of them had called Motheo a whore for being married to a *makwerekwere*, a foreigner.

I tried to resist but my hands were cuffed behind my back and the officer was much bigger and stronger than me. I struggled to breathe. As much as I tried to inhale, no oxygen would come in.

'Here it is! Here it is!' Motheo screamed when she saw my eyes rolling back into my head.

She handed the phone to the officer.

'What's the PIN?'

I was still gasping for air.

'What's the PIN?' the officer shouted and grabbed me by the throat again.

In that moment I realised that this was the day I might die. My survival instinct kicked in and I tried again to wriggle free. The officer's colleague grabbed his arm and he let go. I finally managed to focus on what he was saying and gave him the PIN to my phone. He deleted the photos and videos and even accessed my Facebook app, worried that I might share what had happened on social media. Then he got into the van, asking his colleague to follow him in our car as he drove us to Lyttelton police station.

In the early 1990s I fled war-torn Sudan as a 16-year-old boy after I was abducted by government forces and tortured. After my escape, I made my way south through several African countries over many months, surviving hunger, life on the street, thieves, corrupt border officials and many other dangers to finally make it to South Africa. But today not even my medical degree would save me. I had never been so afraid for my life.

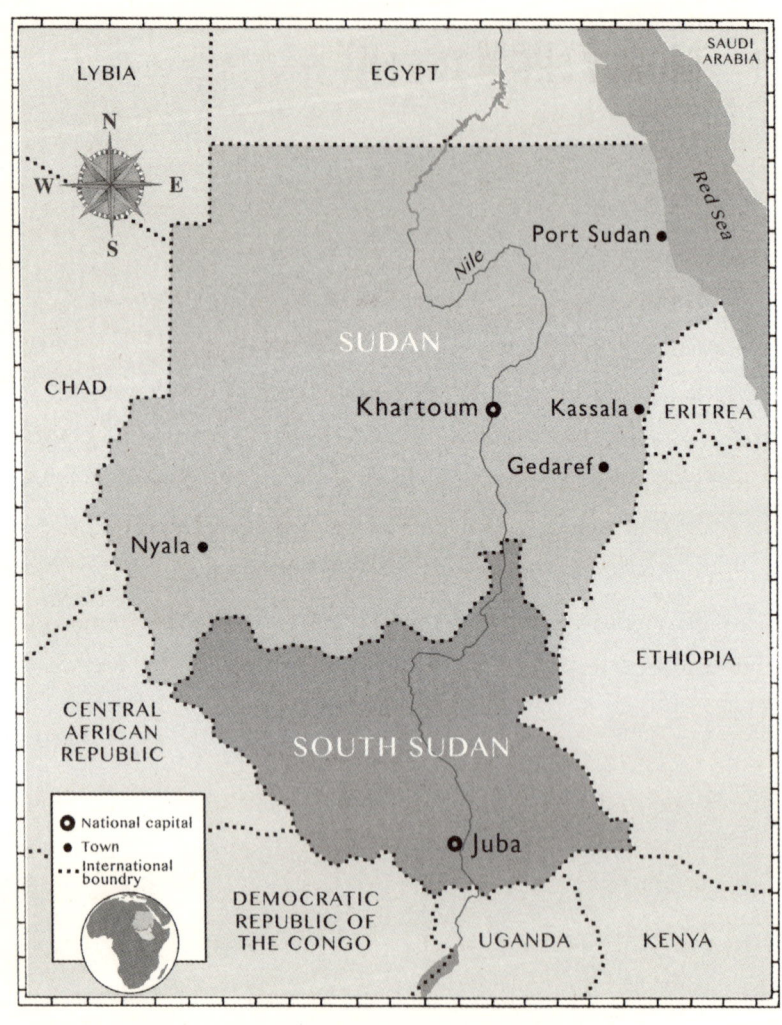

Map of Sudan and South Sudan

1 MONEY FROM THE SKY

As a barefoot boy in the dusty South Sudanese village of Loka Round, I was always running. Nothing could slow me down as I hurtled enthusiastically through childhood, but the pile of money that lay before me in the road brought me to a screeching halt. I had never seen anything like it, so I assumed it must be the sort of miracle, the kind of gift from God, that the grown-ups in my life had always been promising. I snatched it up.

The magical appearance of that money in the dust seemed, at that moment, to suggest that my prayers had been answered, just as the grown-ups always told me they would be.

I was about eight years old and unexpected visitors had arrived at our one-room hut, a simple structure made of mud and grass, like all the others around it. My mother had sent me out to buy a loaf of bread so that we would have something to offer our guests. As always, I set out with all the speed I could muster, running as fast as my legs could carry me so that I could get back as quickly as possible with the loaf and show them what a good and reliable son my mother had raised.

The money, however, caused me to stop and investigate. Counting each worn and grubby note, I carefully shielded my find from any predatory eyes that might be watching from the bushes on either side of the track. I realised it was about $20 worth of local currency, enough to buy any number of loaves, and more money than I had ever seen – or would see again for a long time.

I was so happy that my heart soared in my chest. I pushed the notes into the pocket of my shorts and set off once more on my mission at even greater speed, fearful that someone might have witnessed my good luck and would try to rob me. I couldn't wait to get home and show my mother how the God she told me so much about had decided to bless me.

'God has given you money, Bobeya!' she exclaimed when she saw it. My nickname in the family was Bobeya, which means 'baby' in my mother tongue, Pojulu, a Bari language. The name stuck, even as the years passed and many other babies were born after me, each one increasing the burden on my mother, who struggled to keep them alive long enough for them to become self-sufficient.

For the next few days I doubled and trebled my prayers in the hope that even more free money would drop out of the sky and land at my feet, allowing me to help my mother feed the many empty stomachs that depended on her. It confirmed everything I had heard in church about the goodness of the Lord.

I was still too young to understand that hoping for an un-earned windfall in this way was part of accepting that I was unable to earn money for myself. It was telling me that, in order to prosper, I simply had to pray and then wait for those prayers to be answered. It did not occur to me that there might be another way. Every grown-up I knew was praying for the same thing, and with the same lack of success.

To my disappointment, no more money arrived from the sky. When I thought back a few days later to the night before my windfall, I remembered lying in the dark and hearing drunk people fighting on the road outside our fence. It was not unusual to be woken by such threatening sounds, but it occurred to me that it was probably one of the drunks who had dropped the money in the dark rather than a benevolent heavenly Father.

But still, I reasoned, He had guided me to the spot before anyone else, so maybe He was just moving in 'mysterious ways' like they talked about in church. The incident gave me much food for thought, which my young mind was not yet ready to put into any coherent order, leaving me feeling confused and unsettled. I longed to understand things better.

Typical mud huts in Rajab East village on the outskirts of Juba

Now, after many years of travelling, reading and learning, I understand that the sort of long-term poverty I was born into is not inevitable for anyone, and it has nothing to do with God's will. It wasn't Him that made us poor. In fact, the Republic of South Sudan, as my country is now known, could be one of the richest countries in the world. We have a God-given abundance of oil, gold and other minerals lying under the ground, and our soil is so fertile that it is almost impossible to stop things from growing in it. Yet it is home to some of the poorest people on Earth, people who still live in mud huts like the one I was raised in, with no electricity or running water, and who seldom have enough nutritious food to prevent their stomachs from aching. My people have eyes, but they cannot see the riches of the country. They have accepted their status as victims of their own mentality.

Sudan's development as a country was severely hampered by long periods of civil war, first from 1955 to 1972 and then from 1983 to 2005. South Sudan gained its independence in July 2011, becoming the world's newest sovereign state. The struggle to reach that point, which filled my childhood years, was long and bloody.

Even today, life expectancy in South Sudan is still about half what it should be, partly because of the lack of clean water, basic hygiene, education and effective medical care, and partly because of the country's murderous political history. A country that should be close to paradise more often looks like hell to those who visit or watch from the outside.

I was born on a mud floor in Juba, now the capital of South Sudan, to a single mother in 1977. My statistical chances of surviving into adulthood were never good. But, like all children, I never realised that there was anything I could do to improve the odds beyond offering up prayers to God when instructed to do so, and hoping for at least one miracle to come to my rescue.

I accepted my own helplessness to influence my fate just as everyone around me accepted theirs, and just as the majority of people in South Sudan still do. Because of that acceptance, and because of the strength and goodness of my mother, my early years were happy despite the poverty and adversity that to me seemed normal.

I was the youngest of the four children that my mother had with my father, Lemi Sindani. My mother, Phoebe, was a hard-working woman whose entrepreneurial skills had to compensate for her lack of education and family support. She made a mistake when she married my father, who proved to be an incorrigible philanderer, and they eventually divorced while she was pregnant with me.

Shortly after my birth Phoebe's brothers, my uncles, decided that she should move out of Juba and back to the village of Loka Round in Lainya County, where she had been born and brought up. I suspect that they felt a divorced sister would be less of a responsibility for them if she was safely hidden away from the city. One of my dreams, when I grew old enough to understand the true situation, was to make it up to her for all the suffering she went through on our behalf as she struggled to keep us alive.

Loka Round was about 77 kilometres southwest of Juba and consisted of two churches, a school, a small shop, a carpentry workshop, a clinic and a few mud huts. Our family had a compound of around three hectares on which we grew vegetables, nuts, maize, cassava and beans. Everyone worked together to help grow enough food to survive the regular famines caused by the fighting between the Sudanese People's Liberation Army (SPLA),[1] a guerrilla movement founded in 1983, and the government of Sudan. Under its leader, John Garang de Mabior (1945–2005), the SPLA fought for a secular and multi-ethnic Sudan whose citizens would unify under the one commonality they all shared – being Sudanese.

The graves of my grandfather and my uncle, at the centre of the compound, are now the only things that remain after the village was abandoned and looted in 1986 and the walls of the houses crumbled back into the earth they were made from. My grandfather died soon after our return from Juba, but I can just remember him. He had a limp, and the story told around the evening fires was that when he received a dowry for his eldest daughter, he was supposed to give it to his uncles, who had raised him, but he spent the money instead.

The uncles, who believed that he owed them the money for everything they had spent on him as a boy, were said to have put a curse on him, which resulted in his being knocked off his bicycle by a buck and breaking his hip. As children we were told this cautionary tale to teach us that we should always take notice of what our uncles said to us; if we displeased them and they cursed us we might well end up being punished in a similar way. We listened carefully to the warnings and took them to our hearts.

My grandfather was among the few people from our tribe, the

---

1   Today the South Sudan People's Defence Forces.

Pojulu, to receive a formal education during the 1960s. In many ways, this set him apart from others. He had two daughters, including my mother, and four sons, Manas, Nasona, Martin and Alex, all with the same wife. In the absence of our father, my uncles played a role in my upbringing, even though it was usually unwillingly.

Having sent my mother back to the village, the family built her a simple one-room mud hut with a grass roof in the same compound as her parents. (Many of the mud huts you'll see in South Sudan today are still built the same way they were centuries ago.) Inside, the hut was always dark because the windows were small and did not let in much light. It was often smoky from the candles that we burned for light. The wooden window frames never contained any glass, just metal netting to keep out the bugs.

We entered through a doorway so small it forced us to crouch, and the floor was made from dried cow dung. At Christmas the tradition was to mix cow dung with ash, which creates a white paste. A broad white strip was then painted around the lower end of the hut and the paste was also used to decorate the outside walls with patterns. Outside each hut there was a *gugu*, a round container made from bamboo mesh and cow dung that stood on stilts and was covered by thatch. This was where we'd store mealies and dried meat, mostly goat but also some game.

Cooking was done outside over open fires. There was a borehole at Loka Round Secondary School that supplied water to the whole village. Later we got another, but it was a few kilometres away. We had no sanitation and had to relieve ourselves in the veld, using leaves to clean ourselves. We bathed in a nearby river and also washed our clothes there.

When the weather allowed, most people preferred to sleep on mats on the ground outside, breathing the fresh night air. My mom and I would often lie like that and gaze up at the clear skies above us. Often we would see the planes coming from the south of the continent and heading north. As a young boy I promised her that I would take her to Europe. 'One day I want to sit up there in the plane,' I would tell her.

To some it might seem that we lived in the Stone Age, but I remember a joyful childhood in Loka Round. We didn't have any material possessions, and bicycles were only for the rich – another reason I ran everywhere – but we were very happy kids.

Also living in the compound were my mother's brother, Manas, his wife, Joyce, and their six children. Manas died of pneumonia when I was still small and he was buried next to my grandfather. Manas and Joyce's son, Thomas, whose nickname was Yaka, was the closest to me in age and was to become my best and closest friend in the coming years.

Aunt Joyce, who no doubt had her own demons, would often drink during the evenings and would then weave her way home, stopping outside our house and singing loud songs about us, calling us dogs and all sorts of other derogatory things. This would lure my mother out to argue with her in front of anyone who cared to listen. As a widow of one of the brothers, Aunt Joyce's standing in the family was apparently higher than that of my poor divorced mother.

When we moved from Juba in the late 1970s, my mother started working at the Loka Round Secondary School, where I would start my education a few years later. It was a sturdy stone building with its own playing fields. If it had been allowed to survive it would no doubt have produced many generations of future leaders for South Sudan, but instead it is now just a ruin, the walls slowly being reclaimed by the bush.

My mother got as far as Primary Two (Grade 2) in school, so she could write her name and read a bit, but not much more. We had a Bible in the Bari language that she was able to read to us. Her schooling was cut short by her decision to marry early, whereas some of her siblings went much further. Her one brother, Nasona Stephen, even studied accounting at Makerere University in Uganda and went on to become Commissioner for the Corrections Service in Juba.

The school had been built by the British and included the Episcopal church, where we sometimes went to worship, and soccer fields for us to play on. There was a more basic local village church as well, built from grass and mud, which was where we attended services most often.

My mother was a deeply religious woman. At Christmas, we children would walk from village to village with big drums, spreading the word of God, praying with people and being given nice things to eat. Sometimes we would travel as far as ten kilometres and not get back home till the early hours of the morning. The boys would also go to the local tailor and ask for small pieces of colourful material, which we would then string up in the trees outside our hut. On Christmas Day everyone would gather to feast all night. It was a wonderful time for me because I knew of no other world beyond the village and was simply glad to be alive.

When my mother was growing up in Loka Round in the 1950s, it was a dark and dangerous time. The people who lived in the villages suffered grievously in the civil war that was already raging when the country gained independence from Britain in 1956. From the start the southern states were unhappy about their lack of autonomy, and the fighting went on until 1972 when the South was promised a level of self-government. When the Sudanese government eventually reneged on these promises, the civil war flared up again in 1983.

It must have been particularly frightening for a young woman, for rape was an accepted weapon of suppression and war among soldiers on all sides. When things finally became too dangerous, she, with many thousands of others, abandoned her home and fled south into Uganda in search of safety. It is easy to imagine how susceptible she would have been to any young man who showed her affection and made her promises of marriage and security.

It was in a refugee camp in northern Uganda in the late 1960s that she met my father, who was another South Sudanese refugee from a village no more than seven kilometres from that of my mother's family. His family, being mostly carpenters and tailors, would have been considered to be of lower social status to hers, which may have been why her family did not much approve of him or of the match. She was still only about 17, however, and easily influenced.

I dare say that any romantic dalliance was a welcome distraction from the tedium and discomfort of living in a refugee camp. Any young couple who were known to have been intimate, however, were expected by their families to marry, so I doubt she gave the matter much thought before committing to a path that would bring her and her children much sorrow. She was an intelligent woman with a keen mind for business, but she was not empowered enough to be able to make wise life decisions.

And so the young lovers married and had my brother Joseph, nicknamed Lotola, followed by my sisters, Agnes and Diana. They were all born while my parents were still living in Uganda, but then they moved to Juba and my mother fell pregnant with me. It was at this point that my mother finally had to admit to herself that she had to get out of the marriage. My father was a truck driver who was always away from home. Like many truck drivers, he often had affairs with other women.

Because my mother took the brave decision in Juba that she would be better off without him, and got a divorce, I never really knew my father and he played no part in my upbringing. To all intents and purposes, I was a fatherless child, and I wanted nothing to do with him. I felt no bond and no affection for him. I relied on my mother for everything.

In his adjudication of the divorce, the village chief decided that once I was born I would belong to my mother, as would my sister Diana, who was the next youngest, while Joseph went to live with our father and was left in the care of our paternal grandfather in their village whenever our father was away working. Agnes went to live with our mother's sister, Aunt Esther. Without a father who could be relied on to support us we had become a burden that the family had to share out.

Whenever my father did turn up at our house in the village, which was seldom, he would try to show an interest in me, but I didn't

My older sister Agnes with her children

want anything to do with him and would run away and hide in the bush until he had gone. My older siblings would hang around the house in the hope that he would bring some bread or bananas to hand out to them but I just wanted to get away.

Sometimes he would bring us clothes, but I would refuse to wear them, only wanting to accept things from my mother. I guess I felt rejected by him even though I wouldn't yet have understood what that meant. He didn't seem a violent or frightening man. Like my brother, he appeared to lack self-confidence and had a strange, lazy way of walking that made him look a little simple. On all these visits he and my mother would always argue about the money he should have been giving her to help with our school uniforms and other responsibilities.

It was always exciting when Mom gave us new shoes because

My youngest brother, Kennedy (right), with friends

it meant we were able to run around without being pricked by thorns, but they were only ever slippers or sandals and soon wore out. We also made flip-flops from thick leaves or tyre strips when we could get them.

Mom did everything she could to shoulder her share of the responsibility for her children by selling sandwiches and alcohol in the street market. She worked every day, leaving home in the morning and only returning to us at night, sometimes with a bit of food if she hadn't managed to sell it all. My sister would try to cook during the day, making a sort of soup using porridge and eggs, and in the evenings she and I would sit and talk with our mother as she told us stories and plaited Diana's hair.

Our grandmother, who lived in a hut across the compound, was very kind to us. There were always yams (sweet potatoes) and other vegetables for us in her house and she was probably the only person in the wider family who loved us and did not resent having to help us after my mother divorced my father. She used to make medicine from local plants for anything from headache and chest pain to diarrhoea.

As my grandmother's house gradually melted away in the wind and the rain, the family built her a smaller one on the same plot. At that time, it seemed normal to me that houses had finite life spans, just like animals or people. It didn't occur to me that we should be using bricks or other more durable materials.

Grandma used to take us hunting for flying termites. Everyone in the village was allowed to mark out the giant termite mounds in the surrounding bush as their property and she would always have four or five of them in her name. When the rains came she knew that the termites would be coming out at night and so she would take us hunting. Under her direction we would surround the mounds, which could sometimes be a metre or more in height. We would then set fire to bunches of sticks and wave them around so that the light would attract the termites out of the mound into our traps. When they come out, their wings fell off and they tumbled to the ground.

We collected the termites in buckets. Once we had enough, we would take them home to dry and store so that we could eat them during the winter, when there would be less food on the trees and in the ground. We would cook them in bicarbonate made from the ashes of pumpkin leaves and mash them into a delicious sort of meatball the size of a small fist.

One year we were out on a night-time hunt with Grandma when she suddenly held up her hand.

'Shhh!' she hissed.

We fell silent but heard nothing. Grandma threw a stone towards the sound she had heard and a snake reared up in the light of the flames, rushing towards its hole as we rushed, equally fast and screaming loudly, back home. Snakes were the things we feared the most in the bush.

Every year we would become excited when the grasshoppers arrived because they also made a tasty snack when fried in oil and mashed to a pulp. However, the snakes were just as interested in this food source, and one day a large snake I hadn't spotted darted in and snatched my catch off the skewer while it was still in my hand.

As well as selling alcohol and sandwiches, my mother also got a job looking after the boarders at Loka Round Secondary School. Her duties covered everything from seeing to the children to making the headmaster's tea and running his messages. All through my life I have met people who knew her when they were pupils at the school during those years and remembered the kindness she showed them. She used her meagre salary from the school to hire workers from Uganda before the rainy season to dig and level the ground around the compound so that we could plant our seeds for the following year.

We also had about a dozen goats, which had to be taken out into the bush each day to graze. This was a job for us children and we had to stay constantly alert to stop them from escaping into someone else's crops and causing disputes with the neighbours. We drank their milk, and if a goat became sick we would slaughter it. We had no way of keeping the meat fresh so we would eat the stomach immediately and then hang the rest up to air-dry. The dried meat would be rationed out over the coming months.

Sometimes we would go hunting for small buck or set traps for squirrels and small birds. There were always chickens running around the compound, scratching for worms in the bare earth and laying their eggs in places where we had to search for them, otherwise the snakes would get to them before us. And we could always help ourselves to wild mangoes and guavas from the surrounding trees.

When we had enough fruits to spare we would carry them on our heads to the roadside and sell them to passers-by, waving to the cars to encourage them to stop so that we could conduct our business through the open windows, chattering cheekily, with outstretched hands and pleading eyes.

We didn't have dogs of our own, but sometimes feral packs would come scavenging around the village. We knew they could be infected by rabies and we would have to run for our lives because one bite would be a death sentence. The adults would then hunt them down and kill them with pangas (machetes) if they caught them. There was no other way to stop them.

As I mentioned, I got on particularly well with my cousin Thomas, whom we called Yaka, and we often got into trouble together. One day we were playing together in the family compound and, for some reason I will never understand, Yaka decided to set fire to our grandmother's mud hut.

'What are you doing?' I shouted, horrified as soon as I realised what he was planning, but it was too late to stop the flames from spreading through the dry grass on the roof.

All her meagre possessions were destroyed in the crackling blaze. We ran and hid until it was dark, the flames had been doused and we had grown hungry. The grown-ups blamed both of us and, as was the tradition, a cross was drawn on the ground which we had to step over so that my grandmother would forgive us. Yaka crossed it willingly, but I wasn't going to take the blame for something I hadn't done, and refused to step over. Even then I was showing signs of being stubborn about such matters.

My stubbornness, however, made Aunt Joyce very angry. She didn't believe my mother and her children should even be living in the compound, and I expect she was sure I had led her son astray. I was thoroughly beaten for the incident and it certainly wouldn't be the last time that happened. So I started gaining a reputation with some members of the family for being a troublemaker.

The alcohol that my mother made and sold was called *ciko*. She never allowed us to even taste it, and I wouldn't have wanted to anyway. Sometimes I saw quite educated people, such as teachers, coming to our house late at night and getting drunk on it. I didn't like the aggressive noise they made with their singing in the street and the way they fell about and picked fights with one another over nothing. I couldn't understand why normally dignified grown-ups would want to do something like that. It didn't make sense. Now I can see that it was their way of dealing with the frustrations of their lives, an escape from reality, but it only ever made their problems worse. No one can work or look after a family effectively if they are drunk all the time.

My mother would also bake bread and sell sandwiches topped with beans. Her every waking hour was spent either working or looking after us. She never had a moment's rest, and in her heart she must have been lonely despite the fact that there were always people around, most of them wanting something from her.

When I was about six she fell in love with one of the teachers at the school, a man from the Kuku tribe, and fell pregnant with Kennedy. I witnessed the whole birthing process in the hut. It was a traumatic experience for a small boy to hear his mother screaming in pain and to see so much blood. The picture was carved deep into my memory as I watched Kennedy emerge onto the bare dung floor.

When people ask me today why I work so hard, I tell them that when I was born, like Kennedy, I had no mattress to land on, that I immediately hit my head on the hard floor. I want to make sure that my children all have a soft landing when they arrive in this world. In other words, the poverty that our family experienced over the last few generations must end with me.

I assume that the Kuku teacher was just using my mother, because he made no effort to live with us or to be a good father to Kennedy. On the one hand, I suspect my mother hoped she had found someone who would help her shoulder the burden of parenthood. On the other hand, perhaps she just gave in to the temptation of a moment of pleasure and excitement in a life of otherwise unceasing struggle and loneliness. Since there was virtually no health care available in the area, she had no access to contraception. Even a passing dalliance like this would have offered some warmth and comfort to a young woman who spent every hour of every day working or caring for her children.

A few years later she fell pregnant by another man. He did not stay with her either, so, as far as I know, my sister Sarah never met her father. I didn't like seeing my mother with other men. I guess I was jealous and they made me feel very angry. I remember a man with a limp from a gunshot wound coming round and flirting with her once, touching his crutch suggestively as he talked. I was frightened by what I didn't understand. I was pleased when she picked up a stone and starting beating him until he ran away. I was told she cracked several of his bones and he had to be taken to a hospital, but that may just have been a story that grew with the telling.

2 A STUDIOUS BOY

I started Primary One (Grade 1) at the Loka Round Secondary School in 1985, two years after Sudan's civil war resumed. I never completed the grade due to fighting breaking out and our having to flee to the bush. I turned eight that year. Thankfully, the teachers quickly decided that I was clever enough to be moved forward to Primary Two, which meant that I was in the same class as my older siblings.

Since I was very small, I had a reputation for being a clever kid. My uncle Alex taught me how to count before I went to school, and whenever my uncles came to visit they would ask me to count up to 100 as a party trick long before those in my peer group were able to do such a thing. It was something I was particularly proud of. Furthermore, I had a good memory; for instance, once I was told the name of a bird I would always remember it.

It was great to be in school, and it was well run considering the limited funds the teachers had at their disposal. Even at that age, though, I could see that sometimes the standard of teaching was not very high. I loved mathematics and found it fairly easy, often doing more complex sums than was expected of my grade.

Once a British volunteer came to our classroom with a bag

full of different kinds of nuts. He wanted to teach us their names, but he didn't realise that we already knew the names, as nuts were a staple part of our diet. 'Please don't eat the nuts,' the teacher whispered to us in Bari.

It was the first time I had seen a white person. I wasn't sure whether I should be scared or excited, as my grandmother always told us stories about how whites eat people! Looking back, I realise that this was probably to stop us from going onto the main road and pestering people in cars.

At school we also started to learn English, which I instinctively knew was going to be important to me. I could read a little by then because my mother had always encouraged us to read the Bible, particularly the Book of Proverbs. From the beginning I was always hungry to know more and to learn faster.

The headmaster had a daughter who was a nurse and worked at our local clinic. She was a relative on my father's side of the family and always used to tell me that I was going to 'grow up to be a doctor'. Even though I didn't know what being a doctor entailed, and certainly hadn't ever met one, I was proud to be told I was going to grow up to be something that sounded important. I knew that she was paying me a compliment, and that felt good.

Sadly, the nurse and her husband, who was a cousin of my mother, had a serious argument one day in 1986 and he strangled her in a fit of anger. Such was the casual violence that surrounded our everyday lives. Life was short and brutal for many people, and even as a small boy I was learning that I would have to keep my wits about me, and work hard, if I was going to survive long enough to fulfil the potential that other people seemed to see in me.

Perhaps because so many people in South Sudan meet with violent ends, in the local culture no one ever believes that people die of natural causes; someone or something, such as witchcraft, always has to be to blame. If you are sitting having coffee with a friend and they drop dead, people will blame you and sometimes beat you up – or even kill you – for this imagined crime. People would rather believe in curses and witchcraft, or 'acts of God', than face the fact that premature death can have a natural cause.

Despite the fact that I wasn't learning as much as I wanted, I enjoyed everything about school. I was a true teacher's pet, always putting my hand up either because I knew the answer or to pester the teacher with questions. My early education, however, was not destined to last long because the South Sudanese rebel forces, the SPLA, arrived in the area, bringing chaos and fear.

Many of the SPLA soldiers were from the Dinka tribe, who we had always been taught not to trust as they had a reputation for being violent and ruthless. We were fearful of them even before we witnessed any atrocities. The Dinka can be identified by their facial markings, whereas Equatorians like myself don't have any markings. However, a number of Dinka were also in the government army.

When the soldiers arrived, they attacked a police station in Lainya village, about eight kilometres from Loka Round. They rampaged through the area, taking whatever food and goods they wanted, and kidnapping young girls to be their wives and young boys to be trained as soldiers. Most of the boys would be slaughtered in battle or emotionally and psychologically damaged for life.

The war was impossible for me to understand. Regardless

of the tribes they might come from, any government soldiers I ever saw were South Sudanese, like me, and so were the rebels. I couldn't understand why they were fighting each other or which side we should be on. I felt equally threatened by any man or boy who arrived wearing a uniform and carrying a gun. I did not understand that one side was employed by the Muslim government in North Sudan or that the rebels wanted independence for the largely Christian South.

I heard so many different stories and opinions from the adults around me, none of whom seemed to understand much more than I did. All I knew was that there was a constant danger that we would be killed and the village destroyed by whichever side arrived next with blazing guns and shouting voices, because my mother and the other grown-ups told me so.

'There are a lot of cruel people out there who want to hurt us,' my mother would say when I asked her to explain. 'So when they come, we have to hide.'

During this time we were always alert, listening for the barking of dogs in the night, a sound that had once seemed entirely normal but now was like an early-warning system. We were ready to flee into the bush and hide, sometimes for days on end with nothing but a blanket to lay on the ground and whatever food my mother could forage. Often it would prove to be a false alarm and the dogs would simply be barking at passing wildlife, as they always did, but we could never take the risk.

That caution spared us from witnessing any of the atrocities that I now know were being reported to the rest of the world through the media, but that at the time I didn't know existed and in my innocence couldn't even imagine. Between one and two million Sudanese perished in the civil war, many from starvation and disease. The tribal militias who supported the government destroyed villages they suspected of supporting the SPLA, and would reward themselves by stealing cattle and looting. Thousands of women and children were abducted into servitude and severe famine gripped the land.[1]

Our mother's caution, learned from a lifetime in a danger zone, probably saved our lives many times over. When daylight came after those long nights in the bush, some of the elders would try to sneak back into the villages in search of food while we waited for news that the danger had passed on to threaten someone else.

After the rebels destroyed the police station in Lainya we stayed in the bush for a week, and it became obvious to the adults that it was time for us to leave the area altogether. Anyone who stayed would almost inevitably be killed, raped, kidnapped or recruited.

So we gathered up our goats and headed about 16 kilometres southwest to a village outside Yei, a town in the south close to the borders of Uganda and the Democratic Republic of the Congo (then Zaire), to stay with my mother's sister. We remained there for about two weeks until we heard that it was safe to return because the government troops had retaken the Lainya area. But even though we could return to our home we could not just resume our former lives. The school was now closed and everyone was on edge, fearful and suspicious of their neighbours. By then I had received teaching for only a few months.

---

1   Bridget Conley and Alex de Waal, 'Mass atrocity endings: Documenting declines in civilian fatalities, Sudan 1985–2005', see sites.tufts.edu/atrocityendings/2015/08/07/sudan-2nd-civil-war-darfur/#_ednref5.

After we returned to Loka Round, word reached us that someone had started a rumour that my mother must be a spy for the government in the North because she had been working at a government-funded school. Even the most unsubstantiated rumour could be an instant death sentence if it reached the ears of the South Sudanese rebels or their sympathisers. My mother was acutely aware that it only required one person to believe such a thing and decide to come to the house and murder us all – no questions would be asked. So again we had to flee.

My mother decided to seek protection from her brothers in Juba, a city that was still under the control of government soldiers. This time, however, we had to leave all our goats behind, selling them to neighbours for credit and enough cash to pay a driver to take us into the city. We had nothing other than the clothes we were wearing and a few pots and pans.

By this time, my brother Joseph had joined us. My father's family had not been looking after him well in Mojeö village and he was suffering from malnutrition and other health issues. A woman from the village came to warn my mother that if she didn't take her eldest son away from his grandfather, Joseph would soon die of neglect.

Sadly, it is not unusual to hear of men in South Sudan failing as parents and grandparents and leaving all the hard work and responsibility for child rearing to their wives and the mothers of their illegitimate children. It is another of the factors contributing to our poverty, both economic and social. In a strong society it should be the job of the men to protect, feed and educate the next generation. In South Sudan too many of them have been failing at it for many years.

Our sister Agnes, who had been staying with Aunt Esther on the Ugandan border, had also rejoined us, but Diana and I resented her arrival in our family unit. For some reason we didn't believe that she was our real sister and we beat her up a lot. She was bullied by Joyce's children too and had a terrible time. When children are left to their own devices, without parental supervision, they can be thoughtlessly cruel to one another.

Most of the other villagers had already left the countryside by the time we went to the highway to try to get a lift, and we ended up bumping along on the back of a truck, having paid most of our money to the driver. We headed for Juba, the city where I had been born nine years earlier and where three of my mother's siblings lived: Uncle Martin, a mechanic; Uncle Nasona, the Commissioner of the Corrections Service, who lived in a nice, brick-built government house; and Uncle Alex.

By the end of that 70-kilometre ride, we were covered in dust and aching from being thrown from side to side on top of the driver's other goods. We arrived in Juba around July 1986 with nothing and went to Uncle Martin's house, a mud hut exactly like those we were used to. He and his wife and daughter had lived there until all his new dependants started pouring in from the countryside with no money, no jobs and no way of contributing to the household bills. We were left in no doubt that our presence was an imposition and was deeply resented.

Joyce, Uncle Manas's widow, had already fled to Uncle Martin's house some months before, and her children, including Yaka, were attending school in the city. Being a widow gained Joyce far more support from her brothers-in-law than my poor, divorced mother. Her brothers and their wives all believed that my absent father, who was still very much alive, should be taking care of us. For this reason, they didn't feel they had the same level of responsibility for us as they had for Joyce's fatherless children. By the time we arrived in Juba, I had partially completed Primary One and Two (Grades 1 and 2) but since my uncles didn't make any effort to get me into school quickly, I never completed my Primary Two year.

Uncle Martin was doing well by local standards, with his own workshop and a job as a mechanic for a local church. He had two mud huts in his family compound so there was room for quite a few of us to sleep inside. The city was very hot, though, so we lay outside on grass mats for two or three nights after our arrival.

The family then rented another one-room mud hut a few streets away, from an army general, for Mom and her six children. It was also much like the hut we had left in the village, and I guess Uncle Martin helped her to pay for it because I know she didn't have any money. There were no beds, but my mother managed to get hold of a cotton mattress for us all to share. At least we were off the ground and away from all the tiny creatures that came out at night and liked to burrow into our skins as we slept.

We would all go to bed at the same time, and Mom would tell us stories from the Bible or stories from the village, which offered us some comfort in this strange new world. The move to the city opened my eyes to the ways of the world outside my mother's orbit in the village. It was the end of my happy, carefree childhood and the beginning of my long struggle to survive and prosper.

We had access to a borehole for water, but if we wanted to go to the toilet we had to walk half a kilometre to a piece of wasteland outside the walls of the University of Juba. Hundreds of other people used it for the same purpose, usually finding their way there by moonlight when it was cooler and there were fewer people around. No one bothered to dig a hole or cover up their waste matter as Mom had taught us to do in the village. It felt deeply degrading to be relieving ourselves in full view of the world, trying to pick our way through the foul-smelling leavings of strangers.

We now had no chickens to give us eggs or goats to milk or vegetables to dig up, and no trees offering free mangoes or guavas. There were no termite nests to raid or grasshoppers or buck or squirrels to hunt. So Mom had to buy all our food from market traders, which was a struggle when she had no money.

While she waited for her school job to be transferred to Juba, she continued to sell bean sandwiches by the side of the road and to make alcohol, as she had in the village. The few pennies she earned helped to keep the seven of us from starving. All she needed for the distilling process was a few tin cans in which to boil dates, which she would then leave for a few days to ferment.

In a land with so much poverty, fear and disruption, there is always a market for alcohol if it can help people to forget their troubles, just for a little while. In the end, of course, it merely makes the drinkers even less capable of caring for themselves or their families. Alcohol might numb the pain of poverty in the short term, but in the long term it merely increases the problem. I could understand the wisdom of the Muslim authorities who made it illegal, but the hunger pains in my stomach made me understand that the need for Mom to earn money in any way possible was more pressing than the need to obey the letter of the law.

My biggest concerns were boredom and my desperation to be back in school. I think I already understood that getting an education would be the only way that I would escape the life in which I was now trapped. I could see evidence all around me of young men who left school without qualifications and now had no hope of ever bettering their lives or the lives of those who depended on them. I was determined not to allow myself to become one of them.

For many it was too tempting on hot days to simply sit in the shade and give up trying to do anything useful, but the energy that had fizzed inside me throughout my childhood would not let me rest. It still pushed me to run everywhere and hunt out opportunities for improving our lives. I was also endlessly curious, which meant that I would often innocently stick my nose into dangerous places.

At the start of the new school year in January 1987 I was finally able to enrol at St Joseph's Roman Catholic School, where Yaka already went. The school was run by the Diocese of Juba, but some of our classes were taught by the highly respected Comboni Missionaries, who ran the Comboni Secondary School in Juba. Father Matteo, one of the Combonis, was a big guy with a voluminous beard who was very popular among the children and taught us religion.

The Comboni Missionaries of the Heart of Jesus have a long history in Sudan. In the late 1860s, Bishop Daniele Comboni established some of the institute's first missions. Later several Comboni missionary schools were built across the country and they earned a good reputation; even Muslim children would attend them. The Combonis would play a major role in my life.

My mother somehow managed to scrape together the money to pay the school fees, being determined to do whatever she could to help me develop the academic potential I had demonstrated in primary school. I was deeply grateful because I knew she had not been able to do the same for my siblings. It was as if she was placing all the family's hopes on my shoulders. I was determined not to let her down.

Although I was not required to convert to Catholicism in order to get into St Joseph's, I was happy to do so. I would have happily converted to any religion if it meant that I could get access to a good education.

Despite all the difficulties, my mother was usually able to provide one evening meal a day for us, but it was obvious she was struggling. If I was lucky there was porridge in the morning or green tea with a slice of bread. Having so little to eat would make me light-headed and irritable. On many days there was a burning sensation in my tummy, which would rumble loudly.

Furthermore, the one-room house was proving to be much too small for so many of us. We decided to swallow our pride and ask Uncle Martin if Joseph and I could stay with him, since he had some space in his family compound. To his credit he agreed to give us a home, despite the disapproval of others in the family, who felt that we were increasing the burden on them.

Although I was living under their roof and attending the same school as their son, I was still not treated as an equal member of the family. Yaka and the other children were driven to school each morning but I was told there was no room in Uncle Martin's car for me, so I had to walk the five kilometres there and back every day on my own. I was aware of the unfairness of the arrangement but I would never have protested. I knew how precarious my position was at the bottom of the family pecking order, and how easily my schooling could be terminated if I made their lives any more difficult.

I tried my best to impress Uncle Martin and his wife, who used to call me 'Taxi' because of the speed with which I did everything. If she asked one of us to go to the shop for something the others would always walk there and back at a leisurely pace, but I would always run, even if there was no particular rush. I don't know why that was. I felt I should never waste a minute and I always wanted to show how fast and efficient I was.

None of my mother's sisters-in-law thought that she should be in Juba, believing that she should be wherever her husband was, even though my mother and father had been divorced for ten years by then. And, anyway, my father had a new wife, so there was no chance he was suddenly going to become a responsible parent to any of us.

Although both Joseph and I felt we were being unfairly treated by the family, we never complained. We had been brought up with the story of our grandfather and the curse placed on him by his uncles when he did not repay the debt they believed he owed them. Once he was an adult, my brother eventually repaid our uncles the money he felt our father owed them and freed us once and for all from the risk of a curse.

Later, my little sister, Sarah, went to live with our Uncle Alex and was soon being treated like a servant by his wife. She was given so many domestic chores to perform that she often arrived at school late and ended up being punished for it by the teachers. Thankfully, the headmaster worked out what was happening and told the teachers that it didn't matter what time she arrived; they were to let her into the class and not punish her.

If only our family had shown such kindness, and if only they had seen how important it was for her to get as good an education as possible, rather than simply looking for ways to make their own lives easier. Just like me, she was blamed for everything that went wrong in the house. I went to see her whenever I could, and when I had a little spare money I bought her some cloth in the market so that she could make herself a dress. I knew that the family would never give her anything for herself. Sarah has a strong character, though, and in the end she rebelled against her treatment, went back to live with Mom and put all her effort into her schoolwork.

School was extra exciting for me because St Joseph's was quite famous in Juba, and some of the children's parents were ministers and other important people whom I had sometimes seen on television or in newspaper stories. The children from these privileged backgrounds used to come to school with butter and jam on the bread in their lunch boxes, which was something I had never seen before. They wore new clothes and nice sport shoes, and while I had to carry my school books in my hand, they had schoolbags.

While I noticed the differences between me and the well-off kids, it didn't really bother me much. I didn't yearn for their material possessions. What I did wish for was that I had a father and someone who could help support us. It was in Juba that it struck me for the first time that I was a fatherless child.

Still, I felt proud as I walked through the streets in my yellow shirt and green shorts each day, carrying my books. I was always very competitive in everything I did, always wanting to be first, and I now felt like I was becoming something, showing the world what I was capable of. Primary Three turned out to be my first proper year of uninterrupted schooling.

Despite having missed out on the previous year of schooling, I was among the top two or three pupils in the exams. At the parents' day, where the top performers were announced, there was a hug from the headmaster when I received my award, but no one from my family was there. In fact, I cannot remember my mother ever attending any of my school events. Despite her absence, the acknowledgement I received from my teachers at St Joseph's had a major impact on my life and spurred me on to always do my best. I realised how much I relished being appreciated for the things I did.

In our Primary Three year, Yaka and I would always sit together on the same bench, which we shared with two brothers from a family that had become rich from growing sugar cane. One of them was a bully. He was a big lad and one day he started to abuse Yaka, hitting him on the head with a pen, making him look up and look down.

Then he moved on to me. On the first day this happened, I kept my anger inside, hoping he would just get bored and choose his next victim. The next day, however, when he continued to amuse himself at our expense, I hit him so hard in the face that he fell to the floor. Neither Yaka nor I had any more trouble from him after that.

As the school year progressed it became obvious that the bully's brother was struggling with his studies. Since I was struggling to pay my school fees we came to an arrangement, and he paid me to write his exam papers for him. I would write my own papers first and then exchange and write his. No one on the staff paid us any attention and I still got a mark of 90 per cent, while he scored a respectable 70 per cent. He was so pleased with the result that we kept the arrangement going until we were in Primary Six (Grade 6), at which stage I was among the top five in the entire Equatoria region and he passed with about 60 per cent.

All my mother's children had different strengths and weaknesses. Joseph proved to be skilled with his hands, so he trained as a carpenter. Agnes attended another religious school and Diana didn't want to go to school at all. We didn't yet know which way Kennedy and Sarah would go in life. But from early on my mother made it clear to everyone that she was pinning all her hopes for lifting the family out of poverty on me.

3   LIFE AND DEATH IN JUBA

Uncle Martin used to take good care of the cars belonging to the church, always tinkering with the engines and polishing their gleaming bodywork. Joseph and I were the only ones among the children who ever helped him, but still we were never given any credit for being helpful and we got into trouble all the time. We were constantly blamed for everything that went wrong in the house.

Other relatives used to steal diesel from the cans that Uncle Martin kept in the house and sold by the cupful to people for their lamps. He blamed Joseph and me. Soon we were labelled as thieves and troublemakers. We were never going to be treated as anything other than outsiders from then on. Uncle Nasona also made it known that he did not want us in his house, which had much more room, because he had heard the accusations and believed we would steal things. Life seemed deeply unfair – neither of us had ever stolen anything.

We were never allowed to forget our status as outsiders. When Christmas came around, our cousins would all be given new clothes, yet Joseph and I would receive nothing. Despite all this, Yaka and I remained firm friends when it was just the two of us together.

Sometime in 1988, when I was in Primary Four (Grade 4), representatives from my father's family arrived at Uncle Martin's house to tell us that my father had been killed in an ambush. We weren't even aware that he had joined the SPLA. Hearing the news felt like being told of the death of a stranger, and it had little emotional effect on me. I didn't even carry my father's name, since he had rejected me before I was born, so I felt no great connection or sense of loss.

Uncle Martin was the nearest thing I had to a father but I felt rejected by him, too. Since arriving in Juba all this had made me an unhappy child, but it also made me even more determined to make something worthwhile of my life. Because of our family circumstances, I realised early that I could never rely on other people to be there for me. I knew my mother would always do whatever she could, but there was a limit to what she was capable of in her situation as a poor, single mother with no education.

I had no one I could look up to, go to for practical educational advice or even seek to emulate. I remembered the nurse in the village saying that I would be a doctor one day, but I still had no idea what that involved. The most successful South Sudanese person I was aware of, apart from the politicians and generals who were always strutting around in front of the television cameras, was Professor Taban Lo Liyong.[1] He was a professor of linguistics, a poet and a novelist with strong political views. He had taught all over the world and was always in the news.

My mother would tell me that because I was clever, I would

---

1   While Lo Liyong was raised and studied in Uganda, he was born in a region of South Sudan. He has taught at several universities, including in Kenya, South Africa, Sudan, South Sudan, Japan and Australia.

one day be like him. I was happy to hear that, but I had no idea how he had got to where he was or how to go about emulating him. I just knew that it would help me to find my path in life if I could continue to get as good an education as possible.

One day, when my mother could see no way to raise the money for school fees and clothes for the next term, I went to see my father's brother to throw myself at his mercy and ask for financial help. After my father's death, his house in Juba went to his brother, and my father's new wife had to move back to her own village. My father's brother rented the empty house out, so I knew he had an income.

'Listen,' he said once he had heard my earnest request, 'when you have a brother that dies, like I have, then you will be able to eat his money. This was my brother and so I am not going to give you anything.'

With that he sent me away. Yet again I had been dealt a painful blow by someone who should have had my interests at heart, but I was not completely surprised. I could see why a man who had previously had nothing did not want to share the one small piece of good fortune that had come his way, even if it had only come to him through the death of his brother.

It also helped me to understand why my Uncle Martin resented having to feed me and my siblings when it was hard enough to feed his own family, and why he resented my father and his family for not taking up their fair share of the financial burden. But understanding the situation did not make it any less tough.

I was doing my best to work hard and get an education and all I got back from the grown-ups around me was criticism and rejection, but it had the benefit of making me even more determined to find a way to look after myself and to help as many members of my family as possible. I always tried to argue my case in all these confrontations with my family, and to this day I still fight back ferociously if I think I am being treated unfairly, but there is a limited amount that a penniless young boy can do when he has no one to back him up or support him.

The more I stood up for myself, the more troublesome I was seen as being. I also became a perfectionist in everything I undertook because I was always trying to avoid being criticised and being told that I hadn't done things properly.

About once a week, when the hunger pains became too great, I would make my way back to my mother's house, where my sisters were still living, to see if there was any spare food there. I always received a beating when I got back to my uncle's house after one of those visits.

In 1989, the year I turned 12, my Uncle Alex was abducted by the rebels and treated quite badly in captivity. They wanted to train him to fight but the first chance he got he ran away and went into hiding at Uncle Nasona's house. This brought the civil war even closer to my family and made us fearful of the South Sudanese rebels. It also made us think of them as the enemy.

As my reputation for being a troublemaker grew, the situation at Uncle Martin's house became intolerable, and so towards the end of 1989 Joseph and I went back to living at my mother's hut. All of us slept together on grass mats, just like when we were small. While it was good to be back together again, it wasn't an easy life.

We had a bucket shower rigged up at the back of the hut, so at least we could wash, but since I had so few clothes I was always pulling dirty clothes back onto damp skin, which led to an infestation of jiggers, parasitic fleas that burrowed into my skin around my waist, making me itch all the time for the next two or three years. Then there were the rats that would chew into the flesh of our heels during the night, but these were everyday inconveniences we were used to in a country where basic living conditions never changed for most people.

In 1990 the war intensified, and towards the end of the year the South Sudanese rebels were closing in on the city. The area where we lived was shelled regularly and all the roads in and out of Juba were cut off. Eventually, the only foodstuffs that reached us were emergency supplies brought in on United Nations (UN) cargo planes.

The constant, deafening sound of the shells was terrifying. Whether we lived or died was simply a matter of chance, a roll of the dice. If you just happened to be in the wrong place at the wrong moment you could be killed instantly or lose a limb.

Nothing can prepare you for that noise and the fear that such attacks bring. You never knew where the shells were going to land, so you just had to lie on the floor when you heard them coming and wait as they exploded all around, hoping that they wouldn't land on you or anyone you knew. Sometimes it felt like the attacks would never end, each explosion shaking our bodies to the core and making our ears ring for hours afterwards.

Every second you know that you might be about to die and yet, somehow, you survive each explosion, only to be plunged into the next one, giving your body and mind no time to recover from each shock before receiving another. I still did not understand what the fighting was about, I just knew that the rebels were coming, and that meant danger for everyone. If the shells didn't kill us, then the soldiers that followed them almost certainly would, and the deaths they would inflict would probably be worse than anything a shell might do.

Many Sudanese people fled the country, often crossing the border into Uganda, just as my mother had done as a young woman, but we didn't have anyone who could help us to get away, and we didn't have anyone to go to anyway. However unwelcome we might feel with our family in Juba, at least they were there and at least they had taken us in off the street and kept us from starving. If we went to the refugee camps over the border we would not know a single person and would just become another statistic to be fed by the UN.

At some point the general who owned the hut my mother was renting switched sides and joined the South Sudanese rebels. He and his family were our neighbours. When the government forces heard of this, they sent troops to his house to punish him. The general wasn't there, but his sons, who I often played soccer with and had got to know quite well, were, and so the soldiers decided to execute them.

We heard the shots. I sneaked out to see what was happening. There was a lot of blood, but the bodies were covered by the time I got to the scene. While death wasn't something new to me, this incident made me even more fearful of soldiers. By that stage the government forces were shooting anyone who looked like a Dinka, because that was the tribe most of the rebels came from. It made me feel deeply sad because I knew the general's sons had nothing to do with the rebels.

Despite all the horror and sadness, however, the mayhem in the streets was strangely fascinating to me. Being an inquisitive boy, I found myself wanting to see what dead bodies looked like, and I went to look at them where they had been left lying in the market-place. Many of them had had their heads blown off, while others had their stomachs split open, revealing all their vital organs like a real-life anatomy lesson.

When I was confronted with the sight of an open stomach for the first time, I thought it looked quite like the stomach of a goat or a cow, which we were used to slaughtering. While I was shocked, I was not upset or terrified. I had not realised my own mortality yet, and also, in terms of my Christian upbringing, I was always told that when you die you go to a better place.

What presented a real fear, apart from being shelled or shot or beaten to death, was the threat of starvation. Food was becoming much more expensive and every morning we took bowls to school with us, so that we could each be given a few spoonfuls of porridge by the UN workers. This would have to last us through the day. Often when we got home there was nothing to eat there either, except perhaps a little maize, which had to be boiled to make it edible, and was then mixed with beans.

Sometimes I would be lucky enough to get a second bowl of porridge at school, which I could take home to share among my siblings. The days when we lived in the village and could pick or hunt the food we needed now seemed like a distant dream. The countryside was too dangerous for us to return to, but it was beginning to look as if being in the city was just as dangerous. Our mother was still making and selling alcohol, earning just enough money to keep us all alive and providing people with a means of escape from the reality of the situation for just a few pennies.

I had started Primary Six (Grade 6) in 1990 but our schooling was often disrupted by the fighting. After a few months the schools gave up the struggle and closed down, which meant I had attended school for a little over four years. The constant interruptions to my schooling were very disruptive and disappointing, but I knew that I could not allow them to defeat me in my quest for knowledge.

That year the World Cup was being held in Italy. I used to join the crowds around any television set that was showing a World Cup match. This was the only time I really got even a glimpse of the outside world. There was no way for me to judge what might be happening outside those foreign soccer stadiums, but it seemed to me that the life we were being forced to lead was not inevitable. I was determined to believe there was something else.

In 1990 the security forces arrested the popular Father Joseph Ukelo, who ran the Comboni Secondary School, accusing him of conspiring with the rebels and inciting violence. By then I was nearly 13 and old enough to join the crowd of angry young people who took to the streets in protest, throwing stones at government vehicles and setting light to tyres.

It was exciting for a young boy to join the mob, and to be given licence to vent my anger at all the injustices and difficulties that I felt had been inflicted on me. I didn't understand much of the politics of the situation, but I understood the frustration that everyone felt and the desire for something to change before it was too late for all of us.

Inevitably, I was arbitrarily swept up and arrested by the local police, along with a group of half a dozen of my friends. We were hustled into a van, still wearing our school uniforms because they were the only clothes we had, and thrown into a prison cell that already contained many other people. We all sat on the crowded dirt floor with no blankets or mattresses to ease the discomfort or keep out the cold of the night. There were people all around us from tribes and backgrounds that I had never mixed with before. I kept myself to myself, sitting in a corner and saying nothing, not wanting to attract attention or inadvertently anger someone who might take it out on me physically.

The guards in charge of us had no interest in whether we lived or died. Their goal was to make their own lives as easy as possible. There was nothing for us to eat, apart from whatever our families could bring in, and just a bucket in the corner to serve as a communal toilet. The soldiers just wanted to lock us away and forget we existed so that they could sit in the shade and drink with their friends. If a prisoner died on their watch, the authorities merely shrugged their shoulders and said it was 'the will of God'.

No one questioned the inhumane conditions we were forced to endure, or took responsibility for them, whether inside the cell or outside – more evidence of the learned helplessness, both mental and physical, that enfeebled the population. Everyone accepted that suffering was the normal state of things and concentrated only on limiting their own immediate discomfort.

I can't remember what they accused us of that day. I suspect all they wanted to do was clear the streets and teach us a lesson in the hope that we would stay home the next time there was trouble. As more and more prisoners were brought in, we were crammed tighter and tighter, fighting for enough space to sleep on the bare floor. Most of us were used to living in crowded conditions, but now we were also enveloped in the stench of unwashed bodies and faeces, and suffering increasing pains of hunger and thirst in our empty bellies.

It occurred to me, during the long hours that I sat there, dwelling on my own thoughts, that the God whose 'will' everyone kept telling me this was, was the same God to whom I had attributed the sudden appearance of money on the road many years before. I had been praying just as hard as everyone else in the intervening years, and yet still He had decided that I deserved this.

From the day I was born I had learned how to be helpless, and how to accept whatever life threw at me. I had not questioned the rights or wrongs of what might be happening; I simply continued to live it in the best way I could, choosing to believe the promises the Bible made about the Kingdom of God waiting for poor people like me, and about it being as hard for a rich man to get there as for a camel to pass through the eye of a needle. Only later, once my eyes had been fully opened to how things are in more developed parts of the world, did I realise just how primitive my life was then, and how we had all been conditioned to accept the situation as normal.

I was released after a few days when my mother came to get me. No doubt she had to borrow money in order to bribe someone to get me out. She was very angry with me for getting into trouble and would not listen to my protestations of innocence. She gave me a severe beating for causing her so much anxiety.

She then grabbed my hand, holding it tightly and cutting the skin with a blade, and rubbing salt into the wound to teach me a lesson I would remember. It was not the first time I had received such a punishment from her, and I knew exactly how much it would hurt. I didn't fight back because I believed that I deserved her wrath for adding to the burdens she was already carrying.

For most of the next two years – 1991 and 1992 – there was no schooling. I must have forgotten how much that salt had stung because I was constantly getting into mischief. Now my friends and I had nothing to do from morning to night. We didn't even have a ball to play with, so if we wanted a game of soccer we had to use a lemon, which would soon burst from the impact of our thick-skinned feet and then become useless.

The endless boredom would drag us towards any excitement that would relieve the monotony, whether it was stealing oranges, throwing stones at passers-by or taunting Muslims with lemons during Ramadan. We were fast on our feet and usually able to escape the wrath of our victims, but if they caught us they would beat us half to death, as would my mother whenever she got to hear about any of it.

So often over the decades the schools in South Sudan were destroyed or fighting became too fierce for them to open their doors. Every time that happened, for a few months or a few years, another generation of children was robbed of part or all of their education. Many would get into trouble and end up in prison or be recruited as soldiers and given permission to kill people, while many more simply lost any opportunity they might have had to fulfil their potential and allowed their lives to drift meaninglessly to premature ends.

Clever, ambitious children are of little use to a country if they do not receive an education. It was only by luck that I didn't end up being recruited as a child soldier by one or other of the passing armies. If that had happened I would almost certainly have died before I grew to be a man. If I had been part of a group, and everyone in that group had been recruited, I would probably not have wanted to be left out. That is a frightening thing to know about oneself; at that time I could have been persuaded that becoming a killer was better than the tedium of doing nothing.

While fate saved me from becoming a child soldier, I couldn't save myself from my own foolishness. Our grandmother had also moved to Juba to escape the soldiers in the village, and she also lived in Uncle Martin's compound. I was very close to her and always wanted to be the first to tell her any news that I might hear.

One day I heard the news that my Aunt Esther had died. I wasted no time and ran straight to my grandmother, who I found walking outside. If I had been older and wiser I would have known that she should have been sitting down to receive such terrible news about her daughter, but I couldn't wait to blurt it out. She stumbled and fell from the shock, breaking her hip as she struck the hard ground. There were no facilities in South Sudan for an operation to repair her hip, so from then on she was unable to walk and had to be looked after by the rest of the family.

Since I couldn't go to school, I decided I might as well go

straight to work in order to earn some money for food. I couldn't understand why so many of the young men and boys I knew preferred to do nothing rather than find a way to feed themselves and their families.

I asked around and an Egyptian man agreed to pay me to help him in his shop until the schools reopened and I was able to return to my studies. I enjoyed the feeling of working like a grown-up even though I would only turn 14 that year, but I also knew that unless I managed to find a way to continue my education I would never be able to earn more than the most basic living. I had seen how hard it was for people like my mother to scrape together enough to live.

In June 1991, the South Sudanese rebels again arrived in the streets of Juba. They started by shelling the city, as they had in the past, and then the soldiers poured in, killing brutally and indiscriminately as they went, forcing the government soldiers to run for their lives.

In the international media the civil war was portrayed as a fight between the South Sudanese, who are predominantly Christian, and the North Sudanese, who are Muslim. In the years to come, I would realise this was done to get sympathy from various political groupings and non-governmental organisations in the international community. However, I believe that in reality it was a fight for resources. The South Sudanese didn't have access to economic development because they weren't part of the national government. I suspect a large number of the soldiers on both sides were equally ignorant as to why they were ordered to kill one another. Many of them were simply looking for excuses to loot and rape.

The rebels infiltrated the city in the early hours of the morning, but held the city only for a short while. The following day I heard gunshots outside our hut. I ran outside and saw a group of rebels begin pursued by government soldiers. They were shooting randomly at one another, and the next moment one of the rebels fell. A government soldier walked up to him and calmly pointed his gun at the man's head and pulled the trigger, causing his head to explode in front of my eyes.

None of the soldiers had seen me, but even so, no one cared whether they were being watched by women or children; they just killed whoever they wanted to kill. I scurried back to our hut, my heart crashing in my chest.

As the shells landed and the bullets flew, we all hid in whatever holes we could find. At times I would venture out of my hole to watch the fighting. The rebels held the city for several hours as the government forces regrouped and returned, resulting in ferocious street battles in which many people were killed. Did the rest of the world live in a state of permanent civil war like this? I wondered. Or was it just us?

Once the government soldiers regained control of the city they stormed from house to house, kicking the doors in and searching for rebels, shouting and firing their guns indiscriminately. We knew our turn would come, and sure enough they arrived.

'We are all women in this house!' my mother shouted as they burst in.

'Mom,' I protested, 'I'm a boy!'

The soldiers stared at me for a few frightening seconds and obviously decided I looked too young to be a threat.

Over the following days, whenever we ventured out in search

of food and water, we saw the dead bodies mounting up in every street as the slaughter and retribution continued. Many of those who were still shuffling around were badly wounded.

Within a few days the rebels had regrouped outside the city and resumed their shelling campaign, intent on destroying the government soldiers and not caring how many civilians were killed in the process. It felt as if they would not stop until every house was destroyed and every life ended.

The moment the fighting stopped, we would return to our favourite pastime – playing soccer. Whenever we played a match, a group of us would go around the crowd asking for donations to the team, diverting some of the money we received into paying for our schooling.

During the second half of 1992 I also started working for a market trader, who lent me his bicycle and gave me some money to buy bread for him to sell from his stall. My mother still barely managed to provide for us and I wanted to get us more food, as well as clothes and shoes. I felt pleased with myself for identifying this business opportunity, for having the courage to pursue it and for being trustworthy enough for the trader to give me the money in advance. I welcomed this adult responsibility as an opportunity to replace my father and to help to look after my mother.

My downfall came because I couldn't bear to see people suffering, particularly my own relatives and friends. Instead of taking a share of the profits, I first took home some bread for myself and my family. Then I gave credit to some people because I knew how poor they were, but of course they inevitably 'forgot' to repay me.

It was also not possible for a young boy to cycle around the streets carrying loaves of bread without attracting the attention of thieves. One day three hungry men blocked my passage on the road. In my innocence I stopped, assuming that they wanted to buy bread from me. But they had no plans to pay and simply robbed me of my entire stock. When I reached the market empty-handed and told the trader my tale of woe, he assumed I was lying and that I was just as dishonest as all the people who I claimed had taken advantage of me. He demanded that I pay him back what I owed, and I promised I would.

I didn't tell my mother what had happened but rather persuaded another woman to give me some money so that I could buy and sell bread for her. I used that money to pay back half of what I owed to the first trader. But then I had nothing to give to the woman. In my youthful naivety I hoped that she would see I was trying hard to succeed, and that she would be forgiving, but she was not. I had to run away and hide from her wrath when she found out.

I searched desperately for other ways to earn money to repay what I owed, but I found nothing. Both traders complained to the local chief, demanding their money back. My attempt at becoming an entrepreneur had turned into a disaster. I owed something like $70, with no way to repay it. This incident taught me a valuable lesson: you cannot take out a loan to pay a loan, or go into debt to pay off debt.

The chief found that I was lying and ordered me to settle my debts or go to prison. There was nothing my mother could do to help me because she had no money either, so I was sentenced to three months in prison to teach me a lesson (Sudanese chiefs have the power to send people to prison). I had heard many stories about how bad the main prison was, with prisoners suffering molestation and abuse and sometimes even dying. I guessed it would be much worse than the few uncomfortable days I had already spent in a cell and I was very frightened.

'May I go home first to get my clothes?' I asked once the sentence was passed.

'Very well,' the chief told me, 'but you will be escorted by one of my men who'll take you to prison afterwards.'

When we reached my mother's hut she made tea, and I asked if I could have one last shower. The guard agreed and settled down to drink tea in the hut with her.

Our shower was just a tank of water on a wooden platform outside the hut, with a sheet of plastic nailed up to provide privacy. I did not have any particular plan in mind as I walked outside. It was only once I was under the water and realised the guard was actually going to stay inside the hut that I realised I had an opportunity to escape. Why should I go to prison if I didn't have to? I made an instant decision to run.

I pulled on my shorts and a T-shirt over my wet body. It was not hard for me to wriggle out from under the plastic at the back of the shower. Then I ran as fast as I could in my bare feet. At first, I was running on the dusty road, but once I was out of the city (my mother's place was on the outskirts of Juba) I realised I needed to get away from the road. At any moment the guard might realise what had happened and come after me. I dived into the bush to get out of sight and cover my tracks.

I had no plan and no idea which direction to head in, but I was used to surviving in the bush. I stayed out of sight for a few days, knowing that they would soon give up searching for me. I was only a boy, after all, and my crime was very minor. I knew I couldn't go to the homes of any of my relatives. They would all be angry with me for getting myself into such a difficult situation, and the soldiers were bound to look for me there before anywhere else.

I was not too worried about strangers seeing me in the bush once I was a fair way from home because no one knew what I had done. They would just see a 14-year-old barefoot boy running around, which was not an unusual sight. I was terribly scared, but I knew one thing: I didn't ever want to go back to prison again.

Just outside the city I got to a riverbed where the water had stopped running. There were no houses there because the ground was swampy. I knew that I was safe now because anyone pursuing me would not know which way I had turned. It felt good to be free, but I wasn't sure what I should do next.

In one direction there were houses on the other side of the riverbed, and in the other there was open land. I thought that if anyone was still on my trail they would assume I had run away from the houses, so I swerved and ran across the mud towards them, dodging through the buildings, going non-stop for several hours, putting as many miles and as many turns as possible between me and my possible pursuers.

I came to an army barracks and thought that would be a good place to hide, since no one would expect to find me in such a place. Taking a deep breath, I boldly walked in and asked if they had any work – as if it were the most normal thing in the world to do. An Arab general agreed to take me on; he would put me up and give me food if I cleaned for him. It was fairly common practice at the time to hire young boys as servants. There was another boy working there who became my friend.

The Arab general never asked me about my background or why I was there. But he seemed to trust me quite readily and seemed to relate to me easily. I did his washing and never left the barracks for a month, hiding all the time from the soldiers in the streets outside. In South Sudan it is mostly the men who do the family washing, and my mother had taught me how to wash and iron well enough to please my employer.

I really missed my mother during this time, but I was too ashamed to reach out to her or anyone in my family. I felt I had done something bad and that I should stay away from people.

After a month I felt safe enough to agree to be sent out of the barracks on errands. Two months after running away from home, and several kilometres away from my family's homes, someone who knew about me and my disappearance recognised me when I was sent out to the shops. He followed me back to the barracks and duly informed my Uncle Martin where I was. My mother asked Uncle Martin to come and fetch me because she was frightened what might happen in the long term if I remained a fugitive. So many young boys were recruited to be fighters and ended up forced to commit atrocities that left them mentally scarred for life, or they died in battle; she must have been worried that I would be even more vulnerable if I was homeless and on the run.

'You cannot remain a fugitive, Bobeya,' Uncle Martin told me. 'You have to hand yourself in to the police so that we can pay back the money that you owe and make you a free man again. That is the only way that you will be able to get back into school.'

I could see the sense in what he was saying and I was too respectful of the elders in my family to openly ignore his advice when it was obviously being given with my best interests in mind. I agreed to go with him, even though I knew my family were going to hand me over to the police and that I might well end up back in prison.

The police did indeed put me in a cell, but somehow my mother had managed to raise the money to pay off my debts while I had been in hiding. When I reappeared in court the judge agreed to let me out of prison after just two days, as long as I agreed to stay with my mother. This time she didn't beat me when I got home. Perhaps she thought that I was becoming too old for that sort of discipline, or perhaps she was just relieved that I was safe.

4 ABDUCTION AND TORTURE

In January 1993, after two long years, the schools eventually reopened. It was wonderful to be learning again.

The first day I walked back through the doors of St Joseph's I was told to join Intermediate One (Grade 7), but I soon realised that I was ready to move on from that level. I was worried that if I just did as they told me, I would waste a great deal of time going over lessons that I had already mastered. I was in too much of a hurry, and felt I had already lost too much time, to risk that.

I went to the headmaster and asked to be moved to Intermediate Three (Grade 9). I must have put up a persuasive argument because he agreed to the move and it went well. I never found the work difficult and I always did well in exams because I studied harder than everyone else. I couldn't quite understand why other people around me didn't bother to study when it was obvious that they were going to fail as a result of their laziness.

I revised my mathematics assiduously, even working ahead of the teacher, and I also studied hard at geography. Since we didn't have electricity, I had to do most of my studying during the day rather than at night by candlelight. As a result, I always managed to score between 75 and 90 per cent in the tests and exams, despite the distractions of my outside life and the interruptions to my schooling.

Perhaps I was lucky to have a strong sense of self-discipline and the ability to be able to concentrate on books for long periods. I was always able to sit down and do the work required, which was something my peers seemed to find difficult. Maybe the constant interruptions to their schooling had undermined their belief that they could ever amount to anything.

I passed my Intermediate Three and was accepted into the Comboni Secondary School in January 1994. By then I had had five years of schooling. Going back to school, however, meant that I also had to go back to raising money for school fees. A few weeks into the new school year, Yaka and I went to the Juba airport one Saturday, where we reasoned we were more likely to find people with spare change in their pockets. Our idea was to collect money for our soccer club and use some of it for our schooling, as that had proved a successful money-raising scheme in the past.

We approached a few people and later also spotted a well-known government general called Mobruk who gave us a little money. After Yaka and I had been at the airport for quite a while, we decided to call it a day. We walked out of the terminal building, with Yaka heading in a different direction from me. Then, unexpectedly, General Mobruk drew up in his Land Rover and ordered me to get in. There were two soldiers with him. My heart was racing: what could he want from me? My instinct was to run away, but I knew I wouldn't get far. The soldiers would almost certainly have opened fire.

'What's happening?' I heard Yaka shout as they bundled me

into the vehicle and drove off, but nobody took any notice of him. He ran home with the news that I had been arrested again.

Inside the Land Rover no one spoke to me. I had no idea what was going on. They drove me to the notorious White House, a building where everyone knew that the security forces tortured and murdered political prisoners and anyone whom they suspected of sympathising with the rebels. I was terrified about what lay in store for me inside its thick, dirty concrete walls, with their flaking white-wash. I was 15 going on 16; by this age many Sudanese children had already become child soldiers. Did they want to turn me into one, or did they perhaps suspect me of being one?

I was taken down a flight of stairs into an underground cell that smelled of urine, where I was kept with about seven or eight people. There was no sanitation; we could only relieve ourselves when we were taken outside.

The next morning, soldiers came and dragged me out of the cell and took me to a nearby office that contained two chairs and a table. A single window let in some natural light. Then my inter-rogation started.

'Are you a spy?'

'No!'

'What were you doing at the airport? Who sent you to the airport?'

'I wanted to get some money. I wasn't sent by anyone,' I pleaded.

'Are you part of the rebel forces?'

'No ...'

I told them that I was part of a soccer team and that we collected money to help pay for our schooling, and that we had gone to the airport in the hope of getting more donations. They didn't believe me. I cried a lot. All the time, a soldier stood behind me to make sure I didn't try to fight back or get away.

Over the next four to five weeks I had three interrogators, but the first interrogator was particularly cruel. I never saw General Mobruk again.

I felt very alone. Once you are categorised as a problem child it's easy to be labelled as a troublemaker.

From the questions he kept firing at me, it seemed that my interrogator thought I was a spy for the rebels. To encourage me to talk, he would place pieces of bamboo between my knuckles and between my toes, then squeeze down hard, making me scream from the pain and beg him to stop. They just wanted to hear me confess to something, even if my words weren't true, but I knew that if I made up a confession to get them to stop the torture they would kill me as a punishment for whatever crime I confessed to. I had no choice other than to stick to the truth and endure the pain, believing that eventually they would believe me and give up.

The interrogation sessions went on for three or four hours at a time, with the interrogators shouting the same questions at me over and over again as they crushed my knuckles, refusing to accept my answers. I still bear a scar on one finger. It was one of the most horrible things I have ever had to endure. I reached a point where I became so helpless that I didn't even cry any more and simply started to accept what they were doing to me.

The worst is when you don't know why something is happening to you. Perhaps the toughness of my childhood helped me to be strong enough to withstand what they did to me in that room.

After Yaka told my family that I had been taken away by soldiers, the search for me started. They assumed that I would be taken to a police station or a prison, and so my mother went round to all of them to make inquiries. However, she would never have dared to go near the White House on her own. After about two weeks, an uncle from my mother's side who worked with the Sudanese government forces as a driver located me, and together they came to bring me some food. None of us understood what was happening or why I was there.

We weren't allowed to talk for long and I couldn't give a proper explanation as to why I was imprisoned, since I didn't know myself. I got the sense that my mother possibly thought I had done something to deserve it, and I sensed that I was becoming a burden for her. She didn't offer to try and help me, not that she was in a position to do so anyway.

After being in the White House for just over a month, one of my interrogators, a captain named Hussein, started to become more friendly and conciliatory. It seemed they were finally accepting that I was innocent of whatever crimes they were accusing me of and were now wondering if I might actually be useful to them.

'Are you from Juba?' he asked.

'No,' I replied, 'I am from the Nubian mountains.' (The Nuba range is in the south of present-day Sudan, and my answer implied that I was of northern origin.) I thought it better to lie about my true origins in South Sudan in order to give them as little reason to hate and distrust me as possible.

'So why are you a Christian?'

'My mother was a Christian,' I shrugged, 'so I became the same as her.'

'Would you like to become a Muslim?' he asked.

'Yes,' I said, surprised by the question and eager to please him. I was as willing to convert to Islam as I had been to convert to Catholicism. I was sure that God would understand my reasons. 'I would like to become a Muslim.'

'I will talk to some people,' he said, obviously pleased, 'and see what I can do.'

He must have had influence and he must have believed that I had potential as a convert because a few days later I was released to live with him in his army barracks. There I would start my re-education to become a Muslim and improve my Arabic, the lingua franca of Sudan (especially in the north). I couldn't believe that things could change so totally and so suddenly. It seemed too good to be true.

In the days that followed I became something of an assistant to Captain Hussein. He gave me a Quran and told me that from then on my name would be Nasir. In my heart it certainly did not feel like I had undergone any sort of religious conversion. Agreeing to convert was just a practical way to get out of prison, to be well fed and perhaps to get some lessons as well, since I had not read or learned a single thing since my arrest.

I started memorising passages from the Quran with the same vigour as I studied subjects at school, and given my excellent memory I was soon able to read and quote the Quran fluently. As Captain Hussein was so good to me, I wanted to impress him. After all, for the first time in my life I had breakfast, lunch and supper every day. Hussein was pleased with my progress and gave me clothes as a reward. Whenever he went driving somewhere he took me with him and treated me like a friend rather than just a pupil.

I was even allowed to visit my mother and take her a bit of extra rice. I didn't tell her that I had converted to Islam, and she certainly didn't think to ask. As long as I had people who were looking after me, and I wasn't getting into trouble, she was just happy to see me alive and healthy. As a devout Christian, however, I knew she would not have been pleased to hear the whole story of the deal I had struck with my captors.

A lot of people were brought to the barracks where I was staying in order to be trained as soldiers; nearly all of them were young men who had been recruited from the north, where military service was compulsory. I had plenty of time to become friendly with them and hear their stories. They would tell me that they were being sent to a front line somewhere, and the next time I heard of them it was because they had been killed. I felt sad, knowing that most of them were like me and had no idea who they were fighting for, or why.

Like me, they just wanted to find a way to survive and get food and perhaps enjoy a bit of excitement along the way. Unlike me, they had chosen to fight whereas I had chosen to study, but I was aware that things could easily have been different. I couldn't understand why a government was willing to waste so many young lives, sending people to early deaths rather than harnessing and nurturing their talents and their strengths in order to build a better country for everyone.

After a few weeks in the barracks I was told that because I was doing so well I should go to the capital, Khartoum, to continue my education to become a Muslim. From there, they said, I would be taken to Yemen to complete the process (there have always been strong links between Sudan and Yemen).

When I told my mother that I was going to Khartoum, she did not seem particularly surprised. Many ambitious young men went there to try to make something of their lives in the big city. I still did not tell her why I was going. I think, after all the trouble I had got myself into, she was just relieved to think that I would become someone else's problem for a while.

'When you get there you can stay with relatives,' she told me. I didn't tell her that other people had already decided where I would be staying and who I would be with.

I was flown up to Khartoum in a cargo plane with Captain Hussein and two others. It was the first time I had ever flown. There was no seat for me, so I just squatted among the goods that were being transported. It was exciting to be in the air, but as we walked out of the terminal building I spotted Yaka's sister, Charity. I tried to turn away before she called attention to our relationship and gave away the fact that I was not from the Nubian mountain area, putting us in danger.

'Bobeya!' she shouted, 'Bobeya!'

I had to make a quick decision. If I acknowledged her and she came over to talk to me, Captain Hussein would realise that I had lied and would immediately doubt the sincerity of my conversion to Islam. I kept walking as if the noise she was making was nothing to do with me, but she kept shouting, excited to see me and desperate to catch my attention, assuming that I simply hadn't heard her. There was a Land Cruiser waiting for us, so I walked straight to it, not looking in her direction. I climbed in and breathed a sigh of relief as the doors closed, shutting out the rest of the world.

That evening we crossed the Blue Nile in the Land Cruiser, heading in an easterly direction to reach the *kalwa*, the religious school where I would complete my Muslim training and do my praying. The school was near Gedaref, which was close to the border with Eritrea.

At the *kalwa* I was introduced to other new converts. We were being prepared to become imams in the crusade to convert the Christians in the south of Sudan to Islam. I was back in the sort of mud house I was familiar with from my childhood. The teachers treated all their pupils as equals, even eating at the same table as us, which I guess was designed to make us feel important.

It was nice to be looked after and fed, but after a few weeks in the *kalwa* in Gedaref I felt I had learned all I needed to learn from my teachers. The lessons were becoming very repetitive. I could not see the point in only reading one book and in offering up the same prayers over and over, day in and day out, any more than I could see the point of spending hours in a church praying for God's help rather than going out and working. I believed in God, because that was what I had been taught, but I didn't think that He would want us to spend so much of our time asking him for things. I was pretty sure that He would prefer us to work hard and achieve things for ourselves.

The people in charge of the *kalwa* thought they had won over both my heart and my mind. I realised that although I was now physically safe, I was once more trapped in a life where I would never be able to get a proper education. Consequently, I would never progress any further. I might become the world's greatest expert on the Quran, but nothing more.

I decided that if I still wanted to make something of my life, I had no choice but to run away again. I missed my mother and wanted to go back to South Sudan to be reunited with my family. I had recently seen a map in the back of a Quran and was confident that I knew the route I needed to follow in order to get back to Juba. In my innocence I didn't realise that Gedaref was 1 500 kilometres from Juba and what it would take to cover that distance … on foot.

One day, at three in the afternoon, when everyone else was asleep in the heat of the day, I walked with another boy to an oasis in Gedaref where we collected the water needed for washing before evening prayers. I had hidden a loaf of bread and a bottle of water in my small backpack. When we reached the oasis I waited until I was sure there was no one else in sight before pushing my companion into the water and running as fast as I could through the bush until I came to a main road and his angry shouts faded into the distance.

My heart was thumping in my chest with a mixture of excitement at being free and fear of the dire consequences that I knew would follow if I was caught. I remembered all too vividly the pain of those interrogation sessions in the White House, and I was convinced that I wouldn't be given a second chance to redeem myself. I kept running for as long as my legs and lungs would allow, finally slowing to a steady walk as darkness fell.

I found the road I believed that I needed to get me to Juba, hiding in the bush at the side every time I heard a car or people approaching. I was pretty sure that the *kalwa* would send government soldiers after me and that they would kill me if they found me. They would know that I had betrayed them.

Still, despite the adrenaline coursing through me, or perhaps because of it, I felt like a load had been lifted from my shoulders. I was out in the world on my own and free again to forge my own destiny. What I didn't realise was that I had taken a wrong turn; I was heading east when I was supposed to go in a southwesterly direction to reach Juba.

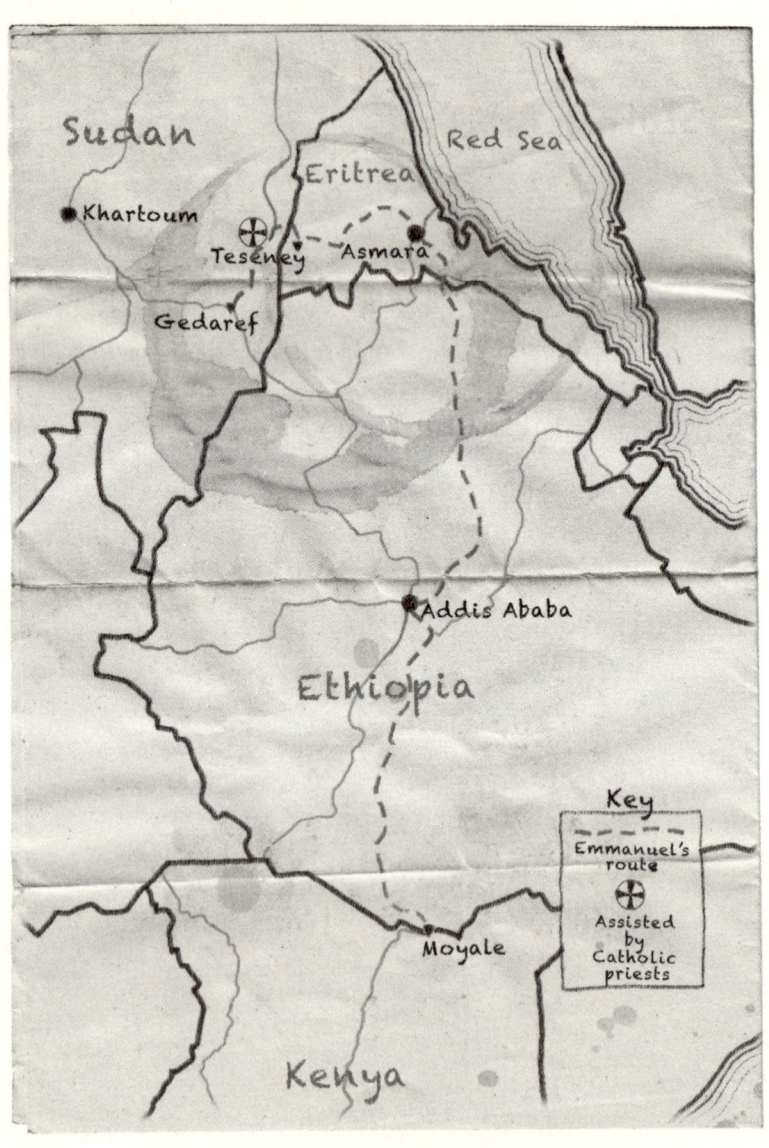

The first leg of my journey: through Eritrea and Ethiopia

5 STUCK IN ASMARA

It wasn't long before my water bottle ran dry. I was able to refill it from the puddles in the road in order to drink, but there was not enough water for me to wash myself. Many of the puddles would have been standing for days in the heat and must have been stagnant. I was worried about falling ill, but thirst overcame me and something must have protected me from possible ill effects. At the time I might still have put that down to the protective powers of God, but now I wonder if perhaps it was just my destiny to survive the many dangers that lay around me.

If I needed to sleep, I simply lay down in the bush, after checking there were no snakes, just as I had done as a child with my mother and siblings. Yet, the risk remained that I could be attacked by wild animals and deadly insects while I slept.

Over the next few days of walking I didn't abide by the limitations of day and night; I simply kept going, sometimes for 24 or even 36 hours at a stretch. During the day I would be in the full sun, but I was used to high temperatures so it didn't slow me down. If I came across other people on the open roads I averted my eyes and never interacted, not knowing where their sympathies might lie or how they would react. Other people, I had discovered, were far more of a threat to my safety than wild animals. I wanted to pass them by like a shadow, an anonymous boy leaving no imprint on their memories.

Looking back now, I can imagine a thousand things that could have gone wrong at any moment and left me dead by the side of the road, riddled with bullets or mauled by wild claws and teeth. But in those early days of the journey, nothing seemed to go wrong. I felt elated by the sudden freedom to follow whatever path I chose. At times it felt like God was actually laying out a platform for me to walk along, removing all the dangers and allowing me to travel safely.

It was as if I was being protected by some force and shown a way forward. I felt no sense of fear and didn't have to think twice about anything beyond putting one foot in front of the other. There was no one to hold me back, no one to question the wisdom of what I was doing. Fortunately, most of the dangerous creatures lurking out of sight were as anxious to avoid me as I was to avoid them, and it seemed that all the soldiers, whether rebel or government, were occupied elsewhere with more important matters than a single lost boy.

After a few days of walking I spotted lights in the distance. It was around three o'clock in the morning and I had no idea where I was, but I knew I was going to have to make contact with other people in a community sooner or later. I could not live in my happy isolation forever. I just had to hope that I had walked far enough from danger and ended up somewhere that would be friendly towards strangers. Having no idea what to expect, I stopped in the bush to sleep, preferring not to meet anyone in the middle of the night, when they might take me for a thief or an enemy before I could explain myself.

The following morning, I progressed with caution. The first person I met was a woman much like my mother, selling tea and bread beside the road. She seemed open and friendly and stared at me with obvious curiosity, as if there was something strange about my appearance. As other people emerged from their houses to go about their daily business, I was surprised at how different they looked from anyone I had seen before. Their skins were lighter and their hair was longer.

I realised then that I must have travelled in the wrong direction. I had no idea where I was or whether I would be welcomed by the locals who were now gathering around to stare at me.

These people, I was soon to discover, were Eritreans. I had crossed a border into another country entirely, one that was only a few years old and about which I knew absolutely nothing. Not only had I arrived with no money, but I also had no passport or identification papers of any sort. Many of the people who came up to me were Eritreans and I was able to talk to them a little in Arabic. They told me I had arrived in a town called Teseney, which meant I had walked more than 250 kilometres.

Eritrea was a revelation to me after living in a country where there had been no meaningful developments or improvements for centuries. Everywhere I looked there were nice houses, tarmac roads and shady tamarind groves. The people were friendly and the food they offered me was good.

I walked around until I came upon a Catholic church and

introduced myself to the priest I found inside. I explained how I had been kidnapped in South Sudan and how they had tried to turn me into a Muslim and how I had run away. I told him that I had been taught at St Joseph's in Juba by a Comboni missionary. He listened intently, nodding wisely. Everyone was being so kind and everything was so clean and orderly.

'You cannot stay here,' the priest warned me once he had heard me out, 'because the Sudanese security forces often come across the border and they are bound to spot you.'

I realised that he was right. As long as I was walking in South Sudan I looked like any other young local boy, but here the darkness of my skin indicated that I was from another place. I was too afraid to return to Sudan, and by now I had a better idea of what a journey back to Juba would entail. I needed time to figure out what to do.

He offered me a bed for the night and the next morning he gave me some money so that I could catch a bus to Asmara, the capital of Eritrea. It felt good to be sitting down for a while instead of walking, but I missed the freedom of the open road and felt a little intimidated by all the people pressing in around me and the noise from fellow travellers. I felt conspicuous, even in the crowd, because I knew from their glances that I looked very different to everyone else and that I was exciting their curiosity.

When I arrived in Asmara I still didn't know where to go or who to ask for help, so I went back to walking around the streets until I found the Franciscan seminary. I knocked on the door, told them a little of my story and asked if they had any work for me so I could earn myself a meal. They were very welcoming and said that, although they did not have room for me to stay, they would show me where to go. I was very grateful and climbed happily into their car after eating. Instead of taking me to a safe place, however, they drove to the police station and handed me over as an illegal immigrant.

Just like that, I found myself back behind bars in a police cell, but this time with no passport or documentation to prove who I was or where I had come from. I felt deeply betrayed. If I couldn't trust priests to help me after hearing my story, who could I trust?

The police cells offered no relief from the hot sun but at least I was given basic food rations. However, there was nowhere to wash and only the ground to lie on. There was no one else there from southern Sudan, but there were quite a few prisoners from Eritrea who had been to northern Sudan and who I was able to converse with. I tried to learn a little of the local language in order to pass the time and be able to communicate.

The other prisoners were much kinder and more supportive towards me than the ones I had shared cells with in Sudan. Most of them had spent some time in North Sudan as refugees during Eritrea's long struggle to win its independence from Ethiopia (1961–1991). Some of them would receive food parcels from home and would voluntarily share their food with me. Otherwise all I would have been given to eat each day was a bowl of lentil soup – just enough nourishment to keep me alive. During this time, I learned to eat much spicier food than I had ever had before.

I wasn't there to be punished because I hadn't done anything wrong. I was just being held while they discussed what to do with a boy with no papers or passport or money. However hard I tried to distract myself, however, the biggest problem was the same as in other prisons; there was no escape from the boredom. Because I was so eager to achieve things, it was torture for me to be forced to do nothing all day long. If living in Sudan had taught me anything, it was that lives were often cut cruelly short, which made it all the more painful to waste so much precious time just sitting in the sun, waiting for someone else to decide what to do with me.

After two months of this tedium, during which no official even came to inquire after me, I thought I was going to lose my mind. I was becoming a permanent resident! To relieve the boredom we would make up games. There was one that involved challenging people to drink as much water as they could. I tried so hard one time I nearly drowned myself. None of these pointless activities made the time pass any faster.

One day I decided to change my tactics. Instead of trying to be as inconspicuous as possible, I tried shouting and screaming hysterically and refusing to eat. I hoped that if I made a nuisance of myself, it would remind them that I was there and they would do something just to be rid of me, but no one took any notice. Everyone had their own problems and worries; they didn't have any spare capacity to worry about an unidentified 16-year-old boy. By the evening I realised the futility of my protest and fell politely silent once more, resigning myself to waiting for whatever fate held in store.

I spent Christmas in the police cell. After four seemingly endless months, they finally released me in early January 1995, with no explanation, and handed me over to officials from the UN, turning me into their problem. The UN put me up in a hotel while they worked out what to do with me.

For the first time I had a bed, fresh bedding, a shower and

even a cupboard all to myself. I couldn't believe my luck. I felt my life had changed for good. I thought that God had answered my prayers and that I'd been delivered from my past sins. It was also the first time I was introduced to running water and a Western-style flush toilet, which took me a while to work out. Was I supposed to sit on it? Stand on it? Squat on it?

It was like I had entered a sort of paradise, but at the same time a sense of sadness crept over me. I had moved forward and discovered this wonderful place, and perhaps I would never want to go back to Sudan and to my mother and family again. All these amazing things also left me a little puzzled. I couldn't understand why things couldn't be like this in Sudan. Why were so many Sudanese still living in mud huts when we could easily bake bricks? Why could we not lay pipes so that we could have clean water running from taps and flushing toilets?

These are questions that still trouble me today, and the only answer I can find is bad leadership. Everyone concentrates on trying to solve abstract political questions about borders and independence, while at the same time satisfying personal ambitions and settling personal grudges, and no one works out how to solve the mundane problems faced by ordinary people. These problems soak up every ounce of their energy so that there is nothing left to create a better future.

While living in a hotel was a great deal better than being stuck inside a prison, it did not solve the problem of how to get an education and get my life back on track.

One day, while trying to distract myself from the boredom, I fell into conversation with an older Eritrean-American man in a restaurant. He had come to visit his family and took a liking to me. When we spoke about my future, he told me that I should 'become a doctor', reminding me of the nurse in the village who had said something similar. He offered to get me into the United States and asked me what I would want to study when I got there. I told him I was thinking of studying political science rather than medicine. His disappointment was written all over his face and he soon wrapped up our conversation and left.

In fact, I didn't really know what studying either medicine or political science entailed. I was still just a half-educated boy with only five years of formal schooling who had no experience of the modern world and what it might have to offer me. I had still never met a doctor but I had heard a lot of people talking about politics and the advantages of becoming a politician.

Above all else, I wanted to learn as much as I possibly could as fast as I possibly could. The slowness of my progress in life, and my inability to do anything about it, was driving me insane.

My case was assigned to a female employee of the UN. I went to see her at the UN offices shortly after being put up in the hotel. She told me that because I was so young, they were nervous about moving me into a refugee camp. At that time, the camps were mostly full of Somalis, not Sudanese. Eventually, however, they decided it was the only option until I could be resettled somewhere like Kenya, Canada, Australia or the United States, all of which sounded like dreams come true.

'How long does resettlement take?' I asked when she told me of the decision.

'Three to five years.'

'No!' I said, horrified at the thought of stagnating in a camp for so long. 'I don't want to go there. I want to find a school. I want to finish my education.'

'If you do that we won't be able to pay for your accommodation,' she warned me. 'You will have to find a way to support yourself.'

I didn't know how I was going to get round that problem, but I was determined to try. There was absolutely no way I was willing to be put into a refugee camp for up to five years. I was sure I would be able to achieve more for myself in that time, so I walked out of the hotel and once more took my chances on my own. Anything was better than sitting around waiting for the system to decide what to do with me.

Back on the streets of Asmara, I met another southern Sudanese guy called James who was a great deal worldlier than me, having already travelled in Lebanon, Israel and Jordan. He listened to my story and took me round to a variety of organisations and charities in the city that he said might be able to help us. It was not an ideal way to raise money, but at that stage I didn't have any other plan so I went with it. We shared whatever money we were able to raise, which was never enough to buy a ticket out of the country but did allow us to stay in some kind of basic accommodation and buy enough food to survive.

We continued treading water like this for several weeks, but it wasn't a solution. I needed to find enough money to reach a country where I could get back into education. Each day I would watch kids in the street going to and from school in their uniforms and longed to be able to join them. I went to the university to ask if I could enrol for a course there, but they asked if I had a high-school certificate, which obviously I didn't, and then sent me away.

Much of the time I wandered round the town with nothing to do, feeling bored and looking for stimulation. At least Asmara was a beautiful city to be in, with many brick buildings in different styles. To me, it felt like I was walking around some European city. There was a photographic studio on the street and I had some pictures taken for the first time. It felt strange to see myself as others saw me.

I even went to the cinema for the first time. I saw Chuck Norris in *The Delta Force*, but I thought it was a true story, not understanding the concept of fiction. I felt very sad for all the people who were killed on the screen. It took me a while before I realised that movies weren't real. I also went to see Ninja and Bollywood movies. The cinemas were nearly always empty during the day and provided a few hours of distraction and shelter from the sun and the tedium.

In April 1995, James and I heard that some southern Sudanese leaders were in Asmara to attend a conference of the National Democratic Alliance (the coalition of groups opposed to the Khartoum government). The SPLA had a liaison office in the city and James often went there for news. We were told that John Garang, the leader of the SPLA, would be attending. Garang had led the SPLA since 1983, and was always in the news when I was a child. I would later learn that he had a master's degree in agricultural economics and a PhD in economics from Iowa State University.

I understood that some of my more distant relatives were also going to be at the conference, so James and I and two Dinka boys we had befriended went to their hotel to see if we could meet them and ask for help in getting our lives back on track. One of the people we met was Dr Samson Kwaje, who was a spokesperson for the SPLA and a distant relative of my father. He had a PhD in agriculture and later became a minister.

It was surprisingly easy to get to talk to Samson. When I told him my name, he immediately knew who my family was. I told him the story of how I had been abducted and tortured and then had to convert to Islam. He was shocked and upset when he heard what had happened to me. Samson decided that the SPLA could use my story to back up their claims that the government abducted people and forced them to convert to Islam. He arranged with his colleague Dr Benjamin Marial Barabas to make a video of me reciting from the Quran.

Samson and Benjamin were very friendly. Afterwards Samson gave me his phone number and told me he was based in Nairobi, while Benjamin said he worked from the SPLA liaison office in Harare, Zimbabwe.

Samson also introduced us to John Garang, who was a big, imposing man from the Dinka tribe with a grey beard and a shiny bald head. He was very gracious and asked each of us what we wanted to do with our lives. He seemed to like talking to young people. Like a true leader, he made each of us feel that he was genuinely interested in us and in hearing our stories. He asked us lots of questions and smiled broadly to put us at our ease. The two Dinka boys told him that they wanted to join his army and fight in the bush, but I told him that I wanted to study.

'Good,' he said, placing a large hand on my shoulder. 'Listen, we all fight our battles in different ways, and by studying you will still be able to help South Sudan.'[1]

Having heard our stories, Garang gave me $500 in cash and the same to James. When we got back to the hotel, however, James denied that he had been given any money and insisted that my $500 was meant to be shared between us. I couldn't believe that he was trying to cheat me so blatantly.

'We were each given our own money,' I insisted, but he knocked me to the floor and beat me until I handed him half of my money.

I felt humiliated and disillusioned. Up to that moment I had thought he was my friend. I also discovered that he had got a local woman pregnant, which made me lose my trust in him even more. It was the end of our friendship, and I was once more on my own.

All was not lost, however. Another member of the group had very kindly given me $150, so I had $400. After much thought, I decided that I would use the money to get to Kenya. I had heard that the people there spoke English, and I believed it would give me the best chance of getting off the streets and back to school. I had first heard about Kenya after my Uncle Nasona had been taken to a hospital there when he fell sick and discovered that there were no doctors in Sudan capable of helping him. That made it seem to me like a place worth going to.

Having decided on my next goal, I caught a bus from the south of Eritrea and crossed the border illegally into Ethiopia, travelling

---

1   Garang was largely responsible for the peace that finally arrived in Sudan in 2005 after an agreement was reached between the SPLA and the government of President Omar Hassan Ahmad al-Bashir. The end of the civil war also allowed South Sudan to declare its independence from Sudan in 2011. A mere three weeks later, Garang was killed in a helicopter crash, clearing the way for Salva Kiir Mayardit to take over the leadership of the SPLA.

to Addis Ababa and then on to Moyale, a town on the border with Kenya. It was a journey of around 2 000 kilometres. Moyale is famous as a centre for smuggling immigrants from Ethiopia and Eritrea into Kenya and, in some cases, on to South Africa.

It was a particularly long journey from Asmara because the buses were old and continually breaking down. The roads were potholed and often blocked by accidents, which would hold us up for many hours. Although I was impatient to get to the new life I was dreaming of, I could do nothing but sit patiently with the other passengers as we waited at one obstacle after another in the hope of progressing a few more kilometres down the road.

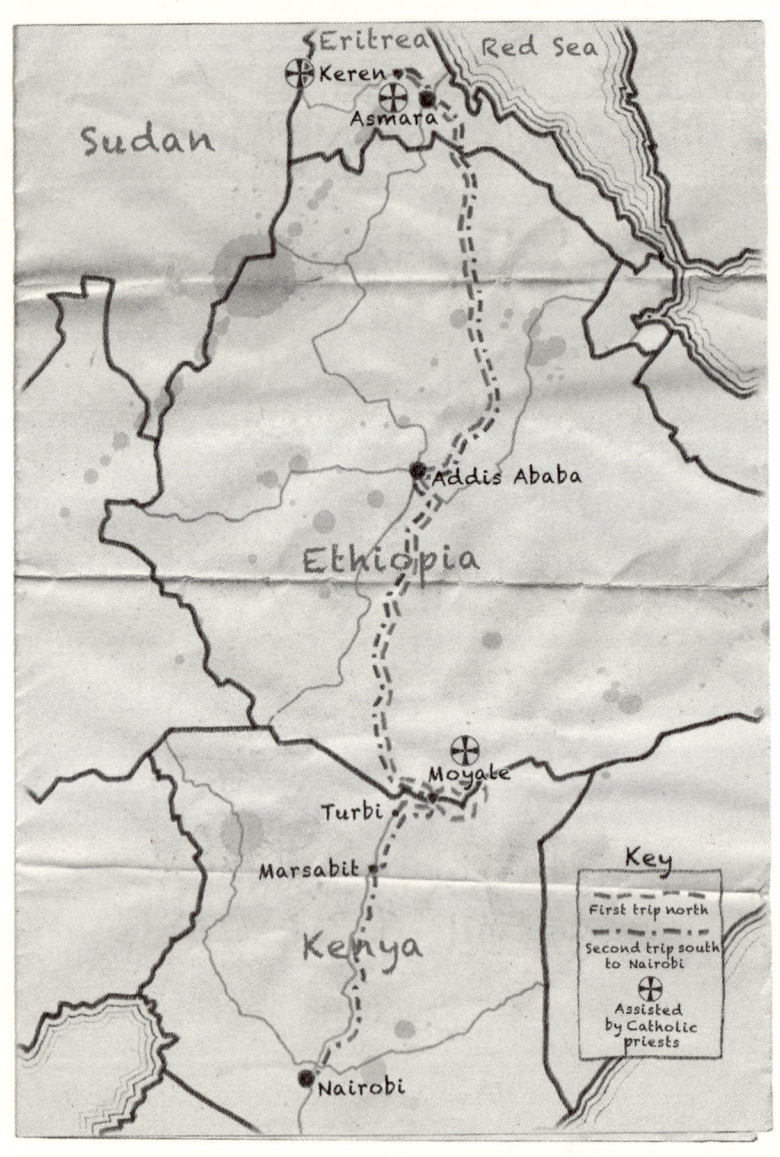

The second leg of my journey: through Eritrea, Ethiopia and Kenya

6 ON THE STREETS OF ADDIS ABABA

By the time I reached Moyale, on the border between Ethiopia and Kenya, I had just $100 in my pocket with which to continue my journey. However, I was told I would need to pay at least $250 to someone to take me to Nairobi, because the journey would involve bribing the police at the border, as I still didn't have a passport or any documentation.

I had to raise the money quickly, otherwise I would end up spending what I had left on food and other necessities and end up even worse off. No matter how hard I thought about it, I couldn't work out how to raise the necessary money for the bribes. I was going to have to take matters into my own hands once more and find my own way across the border. I decided to walk, under cover of darkness, around the edges of the border controls. That way I wouldn't have to pay anyone anything.

I set off at about six that evening, having spent $25 on food and water, following the road from Moyale to Marsabit in Kenya, where I could see the buses going. As darkness fell, the buses stopped running and I was once more walking under the stars on my own.

During my days and nights on the road I had learned to tell

the time by the sounds around me, as well as by the changing light. The stars would disappear around three o'clock, and then I would hear the crowing of cockerels telling me that dawn was approaching, followed by the songs of other birds welcoming the day. Whenever I was moving forward it felt as if the whole universe was helping me, directing me on the right path. At that time I still felt that this was the work of God's invisible hand, that He was helping me because He could see that I was doing my best to help myself.

I felt very happy to be over the border, but at the same time I was frightened of what dangers might lurk unseen around me. I always wanted to keep my thoughts positive. I believed that if I allowed my fears to overwhelm me I would make them come true in some way. I just had to keep moving between the dark trees of the forest that towered above me, too nervous to even stop to empty my bladder.

At midnight, navigating by the light of the moon, which can be almost as bright as daylight in Africa, lost in my own thoughts, it was a few seconds before I noticed that my heart rate had risen dramatically and my palms had become sweaty. I froze to the spot and listened, straining to work out what might have alerted my instincts to danger. Someone or something was approaching.

I jumped into the undergrowth but was spotted by a group of men herding some cows down the road towards me. The only reason I can think of why they would have been doing this in the middle of the night was that they had just stolen them. Obviously nervous that they were about to be attacked by the angry owners, or perhaps robbed by another nocturnal thief, they pulled out guns and started firing into the bush at the point where they had seen me disappear. I dodged behind a tree, hearing the bullets slapping into the bark beside me, aware that I was now encroaching on the territory of the local wildlife, which might well be angered by this disturbance to their peaceful night-time routines and could pose a greater danger to me than the men and their guns. I hardly dared breathe as my eyes scanned the shadows in search of any sign of movement.

Eventually, the men moved away, urging the cows to speed up. Once silence had returned, I waited for about 40 agonising minutes, until the insects started to bite painfully into my private parts, as if urging me to resume my journey. When I finally re-emerged onto the road I ran for several kilometres before slowing to my normal walking pace. I continued walking until seven in the morning, when the sun rose and flooded the scene with warmth.

I had covered around 38 kilometres during the night and found myself on the outskirts of a Kenyan town with my water bottle empty once more and no puddles in sight. The heat was beginning to build and I knew I would soon be in trouble if I didn't find water.

I came across a borehole where a young woman was filling her family's water containers for the day. I nodded a greeting and filled my bottle before getting back on the road. I had walked about five kilometres before I heard the sound of an approaching vehicle. When I turned around, I saw it was a police Land Rover. I ran into the bush but the driver swung off the road and drove after me. I struggled to keep running through the undergrowth that clawed at my bare legs, and soon realised that I wasn't going to be able to get away this time. Panting, I stopped and raised my hands, and allowed them to arrest me. It must have been obvious to the woman at the water hole that I was not from the area and that I didn't speak Swahili. She must have alerted the police to the presence of a ragged young foreigner wandering through their area.

The police took my bag and my remaining $75 and put me in prison once more. In the afternoon they drove me back to Moyale and kept me in a police cell. I discovered that it was a Thursday, which meant I wouldn't be able to get to court until the following Monday, but in Kenya the prison service does not provide any food for inmates. They told me that if I wanted food I would have to buy it.

'My money is in the bag that you took,' I said.

'We can't find your bag,' they told me.

'But I need my money to buy food,' I protested.

'What money?' they replied. 'You never had any money.'

There was no point arguing. They would have become annoyed and beaten me. So for the first day I was not able to find anything to eat. The second day, a big southern Sudanese guy joined me in my cell. He was from my Pojulu tribe, a lawyer by profession who had travelled from India and had, like me, been arrested while trying to get to Kenya. We sat together and I told him my story. Incredibly, he had attended Loka Round Secondary and remembered my mother from his schooldays.

'I don't have any money either,' he told me, 'but I will get us some food, don't worry.'

The next time some visitors brought food for their Kenyan relatives, he simply walked over to them and grabbed as much as possible, fighting off anyone who tried to stop him. He returned with chapattis, which he shared with me, sitting beside me on the floor.

'If the only alternative is to starve to death,' he said when he saw me hesitate to accept the proceeds of such violence, 'then you have to fight for what you need to survive.'

On Monday the guards took me to a courtroom. The judge told me that I must spend a week in prison and after that I would be taken back to Ethiopia. I asked again for the return of my money and my bag, but the prison officers told the judge I was lying and that I had no money and no possessions when I was arrested. It was useless for me to argue. No one was going to believe an itinerant refugee's word against that of the police.

From the courtroom I was taken with other prisoners to a different prison and herded into an open yard, where we were all ordered to strip naked. This had never happened to me before in any of the prisons I had been in. There were people standing all around, just watching what was going on.

'Why do you need me to undress?' I asked the guard, horrified at the thought of such a humiliation.

'It's the law,' he informed me, hitting me hard in the legs with his stick, sending me crumpling to the ground and dislocating my right thumb. I was then dragged back to my feet and my clothes were ripped off, leaving me standing, naked and dehumanised, my thumb joint swollen from the fall. After a while I was given back my clothes and taken to the cell for another week of hell.

True to their word, the police dropped me back over the Ethiopian border at Moyale a week later. I was hungry, dejected and angry, with just a few loose coins left in my pockets. The area was poor and the locals ate little more than bread and eggs, and had nothing to spare for a youngster from a country they knew nothing about. I felt so angry at everyone, including God, who I had always believed was supposed to be my 'shepherd'. I couldn't understand why He was choosing to make me suffer so much when all I was doing was trying to make something of my life.

I still had Samson Kwaje's telephone number in Nairobi. He had been friendly and encouraging at the conference. Perhaps he could help?

Samson picked up the phone when I rang, but the moment he heard my name he put it down again. I tried ringing one more time, putting my last few coins into the payphone, but received the same reaction. Now I had no money and no one else to call on. Samson did not even want to hear what I had to say, probably because he knew that I would ask him for help which he had neither the will nor the capacity to provide.

I understand that there are so many people struggling to survive on the African continent, all of them constantly contacting wealthier relatives and asking for help, and that their relatives can't respond positively to everyone. And I also understand that no one has enough time or money to be able to give to everyone who needs it. But understanding that does not make it any easier to get used to the idea that you are entirely alone in the world, with nobody you can fall back on in an emergency.

I was being taught a valuable lesson and my courage was being tested once again. I was being shown that if I wanted to improve my life, then I had to persevere on my own because I was unlikely to get a helping hand. That lesson has been shown to me continually throughout my life. But I remained optimistic, still determined to keep trying, in the hope of finding someone who would prove to be the exception to the rule.

Samson and I would meet again, but it would be many years later and in very different circumstances.

My goal remained to find an education, but as my friend and guardian angel in the first Kenyan prison had demonstrated, when you are in danger of starving, your immediate priorities have to change. I had to find a way to make some money for food before I could make any new plans for my future, so I walked into a restaurant and managed to find the words to explain that I wanted to work in exchange for food and a floor to sleep on at night. I assured them I would be happy to wash dishes or do whatever else they needed. The guy running the restaurant took pity on me, probably because I was still so young, and agreed to take me on.

I was grateful for the food and shelter, but at the same time I became very anxious that I might end up like this for the rest of my life. At the restaurant in Asmara I had met another southern Sudanese guy, from the Bari tribe. He told me his story and explained how he had been on his way to work in Saudi Arabia when he had his money stolen and became stranded, forced to work at a menial job just to feed himself. He kept saying that all he wanted now was to go home to Sudan, but he couldn't face the shame of admitting failure to his family. He had been there about eight years and to my eyes already looked like an old man.

The thought of spending the rest of my days washing dishes was unbearable, but, like him, I found even worse the thought of returning home and having to admit I had achieved nothing after putting my mother through so much.

As always, I put my feelings aside and worked fast and hard for the restaurant owner, wanting to do a good job but thinking all the time about how I was going to escape back onto my chosen path. After a couple of days, once I had recovered my strength, I decided that I should not give up on my dream of getting to Kenya, however badly it had gone last time. And I must not delay in making another attempt. I had to keep trying, and if I died in the process at least it would be an honourable death. I had to find a way to get past the border controls and into a city where I would be less conspicuously foreign. I decided that it would be better if I went first into Somalia and crossed the border from there.

Taking a full bottle of water and nothing else, I set out once again after work in the evening to walk in an easterly direction towards the Somali border, which was about 390 kilometres away, although I didn't realise it at the time. I had gone about 25 kilometres when a car full of Somalis drew up and asked what I was doing. I was very hungry, my legs were aching and I didn't have the energy to run away. They seemed friendly, so I told them of my plan.

'You can't take this road,' they told me. 'There are rebels and it's not safe. You'll end up getting killed. You won't even be able to find any water. Let us take you back to Moyale.'

I could tell that they were genuinely worried for me, and so I reluctantly agreed that I had acted prematurely and that I needed to think again. I climbed into the car with them and returned to the restaurant, continuing to wash and clean during the day and to sleep on the floor at night.

A few days later, I was told about some Catholic missionaries who lived just eight kilometres away. Despite the fact that the last missionaries I had told my story to had handed me over to the police, I thought it was worth the risk of throwing myself on their mercy and seeing if they would help me. This time, however, I decided I would make up a different story to tell them.

I walked the eight kilometres and was welcomed by a Spanish priest and some other Europeans. I told them that I was on my way to Kenya but the car I was travelling in had overturned and I had lost everything as a result. They were immediately sympathetic and told me to take them to the car so that they could help me get it back on the road. Being a novice in the art of lying, I could think of no reason to stop them and just had to stick to my story and hope something would occur to me as we drove.

Of course there was no car to find, and they soon realised that I had lied. I felt embarrassed and sick to my stomach at the thought of what would probably happen next.

'I'm sorry,' I said, when they confronted me. 'I need your help and I didn't know what to tell you.'

'Don't worry,' they said once I had told them the true story, obviously able to see that I was genuinely upset and regretful about having lied to them. 'We will give you a lift to the bus going to Addis Ababa.'

In light of all the difficulties I was experiencing, I decided to abandoned my plans to get to Kenya for now and head back to Asmara. The Catholic missionaries had offered to give me a lift to the nearest bus stop so that I could catch a bus to Addis Ababa. From there I could make my way back to Asmara. At least in Asmara there were many organisations who were assisting refugees and, also, there weren't as many Sudanese refugees there as in places like Moyale. It would be easier to get help there.

True to their word, the missionaries drove me to the nearest town and gave me enough money for the bus and to buy a little food. I felt humbled by their forgiveness.

When I arrived in Addis Ababa I spent the money in the first day, but several local people took pity and shared their food with me. They seemed very kind compared to the Kenyans I had met, but I still did not have enough money to put a roof over my head. I had to make my home on the streets, even though the nights were cold.

I spent about six weeks living on the streets of Addis, sleeping outside shops. When it rained and was cold I would find some cardboard to cover myself. I hardly noticed the hard pavements or the dirty doorways because I felt that these were just the hardships you should expect when travelling. I had no blanket or pillow, and most days I had to manage without any food. Needless to say, there was no place to wash, so I guess I must have stunk a lot of the time. I didn't care. Dignity was a luxury I could not afford.

Sleeping rough in a city is very different to sleeping out in the bush. In the bush there are the wild animals and the insects to worry about, but in cities the potential danger comes from other people, so I always kept myself private and seldom spoke to other homeless people. A lot of them seemed to have mental problems and no direction in their lives, so what would we have talked about anyway? Just as I had learned in prison, I kept myself to myself during the nights.

During the days there were always places to go to ask for help or food, even if it led to rejection, but during the long nights I just had to concentrate on surviving until the next dawn. When things seemed particularly bleak I would pray for miracles, but they never happened and soon I started to believe they never would.

In my desperation I approached anyone who looked South Sudanese or Sudanese to find out if they could help me. Through this kind of contact I heard that Dr John Tabayi, who was a brother-in-law of my Uncle Alex, worked in the city as a doctor for the UN. I thought, finally a lucky break; God has answered my prayers. Here I had some kind of connection; he must be willing to help me.

I asked around and found which UN building he was working in, which was on the outskirts of the city on the road to the airport. It took me a whole day to walk there, but I couldn't locate the building. I returned the following day and was relieved to find it. I walked up to the security staff at the entrance but they refused to let me in. They gave me a piece of paper and said I should write Dr Tabayi a message. I briefly explained who I was and said I was stranded and needed some help. I decided that all I could do was to wait outside and hope that I might see him when he left with his driver at the end of the day. When I eventually saw him emerge from the compound in the back seat of his car, I ran over, calling out his name, but he didn't even look at me. I felt quite dejected but thought perhaps he didn't see me.

I went back a third day, walking all the way, and again waited for hours outside the building. That afternoon, when Dr Tabayi's car appeared, it seemed as if he had deliberately turned his body away to concentrate on whatever he was reading, as if I was just an embarrassing, anonymous person shouting at the passing traffic. At that moment it occurred to me that the security staff might have turned me away on his instructions, unless he had not received my message at all.

I understood why he did not want to get involved with someone in the position I had got myself into. I knew how thin and dirty I must have looked by then, but that did not make any difference to the feeling of abandonment in my heart.

Once again, a relative was telling me that I was too much trouble to help. I was starting to realise that often help comes not from the people who are close to you or who are family, but from complete strangers. Like Dr Samson Kwaje, I would later meet Dr John Tabayi in very different circumstances.

By now I had accepted that I wouldn't be returning to Sudan any time soon and that I should try to reach a place where I could get an education. I learned to cope with cold or wet nights on the street. I had no blanket or pillow, and often I lay simply on the bare concrete, hugging myself to keep warm.

I might not have known what my ultimate destination would be, but I did know that I was on a journey – and that I would never give up hope of reaching a good destination. That thought kept me going and I could manage without food and without showering most days.

I guess I must often have smelled bad, but I didn't care. Pride was a luxury I could not afford. I could keep going because I had nothing left to lose, but everything to gain.

There was no point in trying to establish myself in Addis, partly because of language difficulties but also because there were just too many poor people around. I could see I was going to get lost in the crowd. Why should the charities or authorities help me when there were so many other people in worse situations?

A lot of what I saw in the city shocked me. On the rare occasions when I managed to get enough money to spend a night in cheap lodgings so that I could wash and get a good night's rest, the owner would invariably offer me the sexual services of young girls, assuming that I must have money. Often the women whose favours they were selling seemed to be their sisters or their daughters. No one appeared to find this arrangement surprising.

Even if I had been tempted, I would have been too scared to do anything, since I knew very well that the poor girls were likely to have HIV/Aids.[1] One of my uncles had died of HIV/Aids in the early 1990s, so I was aware of its deadly impact.

I was growing increasingly weary of the whole business of trying to exist on next to nothing, and so I renewed my efforts to get back to Asmara. By asking questions of anyone with a Sudanese background I came across during the day, I met a man called Dr Luka Monoja, a South Sudanese doctor working for the UN in Addis Ababa. He knew my Uncle Nasona, and I thought he would be the best person for me to approach next.

My perseverance paid off. Luka was willing to listen to my story and to help in any way he could. At the end he gave me 100 birr (R40). Many years later, when he became minister of health in South Sudan, I met him again and thanked him for that gesture of kindness. He had no memory of the incident at all, which suggests that it was just one of many times he helped

---

1   The human immunodeficiency virus (HIV) causes acquired immune deficiency syndrome (Aids).

someone like me in their moment of need. My experiences were teaching me that there are plenty of good people out there in the world, and if you need help you shouldn't give up looking until you find them.

I had been in Addis Ababa for about two months when I left the city for Asmara, using the money Luka gave me to take a bus to the Tigray region, in northern Ethiopia. I put out of my mind how far and how expensive the journey from there to Eritrea was bound to be and took it one town at a time, searching at each stop for ways to make enough money to buy a bus ticket to the next or, failing that, just keeping on walking. I often went to Catholic churches and found the priests willing to assist me, even if it was just with some food or a little money.

When I arrived in Tigray, the priests at a Catholic church told me about some Comboni nuns who lived between Asmara and Keren, to the north of the Eritrean capital. I decided that Keren would be my next destination.

When I got to the Comboni nuns they introduced me to Sister Else, who had worked in Sudan as a Comboni sister for a few years and so understood what it was that I was escaping from. My money had run out again by that stage and I needed a place to stay, so I asked the nuns if I could work for them in return for board and lodging. They kindly agreed.

I stayed for a week and Sister Else offered to write a letter of introduction for me to the Bishop of Caritas Eritrea, the Catholic Secretariat, in Asmara. On the strength of her letter the Bishop received me, listened to my story and gave me $500.

This was to prove to be my best break so far, but it would not have happened if I had not suffered all the previous setbacks and kept going, following a path that eventually brought me to the kind Bishop's door. Suddenly my dream of getting to Kenya was a realistic possibility again. It was like a sign, telling me that however hard it might seem, and however convoluted the journey might be, I was on the right path to my destiny.

Someone among the many people I had talked to over the previous months had told me that if I wanted to get into Kenya, I needed to buy an Ethiopian passport. If you had one then you didn't need any sort of visa. Up till then I had been travelling with no identity papers of any sort, which was one of the main problems in trying to pass from one country to another. I was a man without any formal identity, adrift in the world like a piece of human flotsam on the ocean.

I duly returned to Addis and went to the immigration centre, where I knew I would find people outside selling passports. I used $100 of the Bishop's money to buy a passport from an 18-year-old girl called Ababa, a name that I thought would work for a boy just as well as a girl as far as the border officials were concerned. I replaced her picture with mine, took a bus to Moyale and crossed the border into Kenya like any legal traveller.

This time I had my fake passport stamped with no trouble at all. It seemed I now had an identity, at least as far as the outside world was concerned, even though it wasn't the one I had been born with.

The third leg of my journey: from Kenya to South Africa

100

7 FIGHTING OFF THIEVES AND SNAKES

Once I reached Nairobi around the end of May 1995, my confidence rising once more, I phoned one of my relatives in Nairobi and asked them to call another distant relative, Dr Thomas Taban, who was a veterinarian. I had heard he was working for the UN in Somalia but was based in the Kenyan capital with his family. The call was made and Dr Taban invited me to his house to meet his family. I ended up staying for three days, at the end of which the doctor called a family meeting at ten in the morning and asked me what my plan was. I had no answer to give him so I remained silent.

I had a feeling that if I had been the son of one of my uncles he would have helped me, but like the other men in the family, he felt that I should be the responsibility of my father's family. Over the previous three days he had obviously grown concerned that he would have to take me on. The prospect of having to support someone who was a relative stranger to his family had obviously panicked him.

'I can't afford to support you to live here,' he told me bluntly, 'so if you do not have a plan you will have to go to the refugee camp and apply for resettlement.'

I was shocked but tried to hide my feelings and behave like a grown-up. I couldn't imagine why any adult would think it was a good idea to send a young boy to a camp where he knew no one and where he would receive no education. I can only assume he must have thought I was older.

'How long do people have to wait for resettlement?' I asked as I had of the UN officer in Asmara about a year before.

'Three to five years.'

It was the same answer, and it filled me with exactly the same level of horror. There was no way I was willing to risk wasting that much time before resuming my education, but I felt I had to come up with a credible plan for the doctor in case he informed the authorities about me and I ended up back in prison. If he wasn't going to help me, then I had no one else to turn to in Kenya. I had to come up with an alternative.

The evening before, I had bought a Coke and had noticed that it was made in South Africa. I was surprised that Coke was not produced locally in Kenya. That thought still lingered in my head.

'I am going to go to South Africa,' I told him.

'Okay,' he said, obviously surprised. 'When are you going to South Africa?'

'Today.'

'You are going today but you didn't want to tell me?'

'I was going to tell you,' I said, not wanting to admit that I had only just thought of it.

'Okay. Do you have enough money?'

'Yes,' I said, knowing that I was now down to my last $50. 'I have money.'

He gave me another $50, which was kind of him and probably made him feel a bit better. I headed back to the bus station, feeling tearful and angry at having been rejected for a third time, and still the rooster did not crow. I didn't know exactly where I was going to end up, but I was determined to create my own identity in the world so that I would have some control over my own fate.

After so many months on the road, I had seen and experienced so much. Even though it was incredibly tough at times, I realised that there was a bigger world out there. There was nothing left for me in Juba but my poor mother. I'd met so many Sudanese on the road and felt it would be stupid of me to return to my home country when so many people were leaving it.

I also needed to define myself as someone who was not dependent on anyone. Even if I had to work as a slave, I would do anything to be able to stand on my own and not have to rely on anyone. Up to this point, my journey had taught me that perseverance is the only key for overcoming hardship and rejection.

I knew next to nothing about South Africa except what we had learned in history about Lord Kitchener, who had fought in the Anglo-Boer War (1899–1902) after defeating the Mahdi in Sudan in 1898. I didn't know anything about all the white people living there or about the cruel laws of apartheid. The only white people I had met up till then had been missionaries and aid workers, who seemed to be kind people even if they hadn't all been exactly helpful.

I had a map, which told me that this time I would have to travel about 4 000 kilometres. On paper it looked doable, but the way things look on a map is very different from the reality of standing on the roadside looking at the distant horizon. I could see that from

Kenya I would need to head first to Dar es Salaam in Tanzania via Arusha, then on through Mozambique. I didn't care how far it was or how long it was going to take me but I could see that it was going to be hard to make $100 last for such a long journey.

I was 17 when I left Nairobi for South Africa in May 1995. The bus left at seven in the evening. My first ticket, taking me as far as Dar es Salaam on the Tanzanian coast, cost $60, leaving me with just $40. Once I arrived there, I was told that my second ticket, which would take me on to Mtwara in southern Tanzania, would cost another $50. I couldn't afford it, so I spent a few days begging for work in exchange for food and a place to sleep in the restaurants of Dar es Salaam, offering to do any kind of work anyone had to offer, sleeping on the streets and trying desperately not to spend any more of my money while I worked out what to do next. When I came across a Catholic church I went inside to talk to the priest. He felt sorry for me and gave me all the money he could spare, which was about $20. By then I needed to buy food, so I still didn't have enough to pay for my ticket out.

Eventually, however, I raised the funds by doing odd jobs and made it down to the Ruvuma River, which separates Tanzania and Mozambique and empties into the Indian Ocean. There I ran out of money again. As I stood on the shore staring across to the other side, it seemed ridiculous that I couldn't afford to make such a short journey.

'I think I can swim that,' I said to myself. 'It's like walking, just a question of keeping going and not giving up.'

Having made up my mind, I plunged straight into the river's

fast-flowing waters. I had only taken a few strokes, however, when a herd of hippos lifted their eyes menacingly from the water and stared at me. I knew exactly how dangerous they could be from the many stories I had heard around fires in my childhood, and I also knew that if I got too far from the shore I would never be able to out-swim them should they decide to come after me.

Filled with the same surge of panic I used to feel as a child when confronted by a snake in the bush, I immediately turned around and quickly swam back to shore, my heart crashing in my chest as I pulled myself onto dry land. They continued to stare.

'Where are you going?' A passer-by asked as I sat, panting, on the side, watching the giant animals wallowing in front of me, daring me to trespass on their territory again.

'To the other side,' I said, pointing across the water. 'It's just there. I can see the road I want to follow when I get there.'

'You can't go now,' he said. 'It's four in the afternoon and it's too far and too dangerous.'

'No,' I shook my head. 'I'm going.'

'Okay,' he said. 'Well, I have a boat and if you pay me I will get you across.'

'I've only got $10,' I said.

'Okay,' he said after a moment's thought. I handed over the money, hoping that I wasn't about to be robbed. He then fetched his boat and ferried me safely across, past the silently watching hippos.

Once I got to the other side, I thanked the boatman and set off on the next leg of my journey. I had been walking only for an hour or two when my heart rate rose and my palms began to sweat once more. I froze, aware that this meant there was danger nearby, and heard a terrible hissing sound. Ahead of me on the path were two black mambas fighting over the corpse of a rat. Being terrified of snakes ever since I was old enough to walk, I just stared, poised to run, as I waited for them to finish their battle and move away.

It often occurred to me on my travels that if something happened to me and I died by the side of the road, no one would ever know who I was. I had no identity papers apart from the fake passport I had bought in Addis. I would just have been an anonymous body and my mother would never have discovered my fate. If I was lucky, some stranger would dig me a shallow grave for my final resting place. Since I often went several days without seeing anyone, I might not even be found before my body decomposed or was eaten by animals. It would be as if I had never existed.

It felt like I was there for hours, but the black mambas – whose venom can kill you in minutes – didn't seem in any hurry to go. I decided I must be braver and gathered up some stones to throw at them. To my surprise they immediately disappeared into the undergrowth, but as I walked cautiously forward one of them suddenly reappeared and slithered between my legs, I galloped forwards, unsure if it had bitten me as it passed.

Once I was sure I was clear of the snakes, and was confident I hadn't been bitten, I resumed my normal steady pace. I kept it up till three in the morning, at which point I came upon a big old mango tree beside a small fishing boat upturned on a beach. I was in northern Mozambique, at a village near the town of Mocímboa da Praia. Looking around, I could see no sign of people anywhere. The night was hot and I decided that I needed to take the opportunity to rest. I lay down beneath the tree and closed my eyes, immediately lulled into a deep sleep by the steady sound of the waves on the sand.

I must have been exhausted that night because I did not wake when the sun rose, but in my dreams I heard people whispering in a strange language. The voices grew louder and when I eventually opened my eyes, squinting into the brightness of the day, I found myself surrounded by a crowd of curious locals. I let out a scream of shock and they all hurried to reassure me that they meant me no harm. I realised they were speaking Portuguese and that I was so scared I had actually wet my trousers.

'Please don't hurt me,' I cried. I doubt they understood but they took pity, calmed me and brought me bread and tea.

The villagers didn't speak any English or Arabic, but I managed to convey that I wanted to get to Maputo, the capital of Mozambique, and they pointed me towards the best road. They asked via sign language if I had any money and I was able to show them my empty pockets. They looked after me and fed me for the rest of the day, and that evening, feeling well rested, I set out once more to follow the road. Encouraged by the friendliness of the people – a pleasant change after the unhelpfulness of some of my own family members – I stopped to sleep again in the next village that I reached.

When I woke the next day, the people told me about some Comboni nuns in a village to the north of Nampula who they said would be willing to help me. The nuns kindly gave me some food and a little money to get to Nampula, where they said I would find some Comboni Fathers who would help me. Always keen to make use of any personal introductions I was lucky enough to be given, I did as they suggested.

In Nampula I was received by an Italian priest called Father Joseph. I told my story yet again. Father Joseph told me that he was just back from visiting the Comboni Mission in Johannesburg. It turned out that he had met two South Sudanese priests at the mission; one was none other than Father Joseph Ukelo, who had been the head of Comboni Secondary School in Juba and whose arrest had led to the street protests during which I was arrested. The other was Father Albino Adot, who used to work at St Kizito School in Juba, against whom we often played soccer games.

Even though I'd only heard of them before, I told Father Joseph that I knew the two priests. He decided to call the mission in Johannesburg to check, as Father Albino was still there. Father Albino didn't know me personally, but he kindly vouched for me as a fellow countryman.

Father Joseph very generously gave me $400 to travel to Maputo, which I divided carefully between my pockets and my bag. Yet again a Comboni missionary had come to my rescue.

When I went looking for transport, I found the owner of a truck who told me he was going to Maputo. He invited me to sit in the cabin of the truck and wait for the driver.

'Give me your bag,' he said as I climbed in, 'there's no space for it in there. I'll put it in the back.'

I handed him the bag and made myself comfortable in the passenger seat. A few moments later the driver, a different man, climbed in and looked at me angrily.

'What are you doing in my truck?' he demanded.

'The owner of the truck told me that you would drive me to Maputo,' I protested.

'I'm not going to Maputo!' He shouted. 'Get out of my truck!'

I immediately realised that I had been scammed and my bag was gone. I had lost most of the money Father Joseph had just given me, along with my few worldly possessions, including my fake passport and the photographs of myself that I had had taken in Asmara. The only thing I still had on me was my pocket New Testament.

I have never felt so angry, both at the man who had robbed me and at myself for once again being too trusting and allowing myself to be so easily fooled. There was nothing I could do. The man had disappeared and my money and possessions had gone with him, leaving me fuming on the side of the road and searching for another way to continue.

In trying to find a ride for the next stage of my journey, I got to talk to a lot of people from Ethiopia and Eritrea who were also heading for South Africa. Many of them told me that they were going to go via the Komatipoort border post. I decided that it would be a better idea to choose a less obvious route and deviate through Zimbabwe, where I believed my chances of getting across would be improved. I was still little more than a teenager and I knew that would make me conspicuous to border officials.

Using the money I had concealed in the pockets of my shorts, I made my way by bus first to Chimoio and then across the border to Mutare in Zimbabwe. It was a porous border, and to my relief I easily found a place to slip across. I still had some money left from Father Joseph, which I used to buy a bus ticket to the capital, Harare. I knew that there was a liaison office for the South Sudanese rebel movement in Harare that was run by Dr Benjamin Marial Barabas, whom I had met at the SPLA conference in Asmara several months before. I asked him to write me a letter confirming that I was Sudanese as some form of identification and asking people to help me wherever possible. That same evening, I took a train down to the South African border post at Beitbridge, arriving in the middle of the afternoon.

I noticed a Catholic church in Beitbridge and went inside, where I spotted a priest. I asked for his help, since I had very little money left. He gave me R100.

Taking a deep breath, I started walking towards the border.

'Where are you going?' a Zimbabwean customs officer challenged me.

'I'm going to South Africa,' I replied, as if it were the most normal thing in the world to do.

'Where are you from?' he demanded.

'Southern Sudan.'

'Do you have a visa?'

'No, I don't.'

'Then you can't go or they will put you in prison. Do you want to go to prison?'

'No,' I said, remembering the various prison cells I had already endured on my journey.

'Come and stay with me,' he said. 'I'll help you to go across tomorrow.'

'I've only got R100 and $50 left,' I said.

'That's fine,' he said, 'I don't need your money.'

Despite my recent experience, I didn't think I had an alternative. He seemed trustworthy and I couldn't come up with a better option, so I agreed. He took me to his home, which was a one-bedroom studio apartment, gave me something to eat and let me sleep on his couch.

In the morning I decided to trust him, despite everything that had happened to me along the way, and gave him my R100. He walked me across the border to the South African side – no one stopped us or even looked at us suspiciously – and put me in a taxi, telling the driver to take me to Johannesburg, and he paid him. The driver even gave me some change.

It was as easy as that.

Today I sometimes wonder how I managed to travel all those thousands of kilometres virtually penniless. Was it God, the universe or pure luck? But, whatever it is, I'm very grateful for it. What must have helped was that I was still quite young and people seemed to take pity on me. For one, there was the golden thread of the various Comboni missionaries and nuns, as well as other Catholic clergymen, who helped me along the way. But, also, I was never afraid to take the first step and take responsibility for my own destiny.

8   A HOME WITH THE COMBONIS

About 18 months after I left Juba for Khartoum with Captain Hussein, I arrived in Johannesburg in the early evening, crammed into one of the many minibus taxis that seemed to be stopping and starting at every roadside. I could hardly believe my eyes. I had never seen roads this smooth and wide enough to carry four vehicles in the same direction. The streetlights and buildings towered above us and headlights poured towards us.

We were part of a spectacular light show as streams of cars sped around us, zig-zagging from lane to lane, their red brake lights snaking away into the distance. There were so many beautiful, clean cars, all of them reflecting the lights from their shiny paintwork and none of them emitting the clouds of black exhaust smoke I was used to. There was so much speed and light and activity that I was simultaneously dazed and afraid, excited and overwhelmed. It was towards the end of August 1995; I was about a month away from my 18th birthday.

I had no contacts or addresses in the city, so I had no idea where I should get off. The centre of the city was much cleaner and better maintained than it is today and I made the decision to climb out with the other passengers at a 50-storey skyscraper and shopping centre called the Carlton Centre. It looked so smart as I stood below it that I assumed I would need permission to go inside. I couldn't believe it when I discovered that I was allowed to just walk through the doors like everyone else. In front of me was a gleaming escalator, something I had never seen before. I stood and watched people jumping on and off for a few minutes before plucking up the courage to do the same. It was a wonderful feeling to be lifted effortlessly up to the next floor, surrounded by so many prosperous-looking people.

I was wearing my only shirt and my only pair of trousers and had not showered since leaving the customs officer's flat at Beitbridge. I badly needed to wash. Once back on the street I walked around for a while until I found the Nugget Hotel, where bed and breakfast for one night was just $20, which was exactly what I had left in my pocket. It felt good to be able to take a shower and lie on a proper bed for a few hours. After breakfast the next day, however, I knew I would be starting out on my new life with nothing once again.

I remembered how kind and helpful Father Joseph had been to me in Mozambique, and I spent the day trying to track down a phone number for the Comboni Missionaries in Johannesburg in the hope of finding them again, but with no success. The next night I had to sleep outside because I had no money left. A guy I met on the street invited me to come back with him to the famous township of Soweto. I walked with him for a bit, but then I got a bad feeling. After my experiences on the road, I was reluctant to trust anyone. Furthermore, I felt my chances of finding opportunities were much better if I stayed in the city centre.

Looking for somewhere to sleep, I found a small park, but it seemed too exposed. There weren't as many homeless people as in the other cities I had lived in, and I felt it would be a bad idea to be either too conspicuous or too hidden. The other homeless people I saw seemed to be drunk or on drugs. Some of them seemed angry, fighting and shouting with one another over some scrap of a possession or perhaps over nothing at all.

By this stage I had been living as a street child for over a year. I had been outside in Addis Ababa during the rainy season and in Tigray, Dar es Salaam and all over Mozambique, eking out whatever money I might have so that I was always left with enough to eat and to stay alive. There were so many other people on the streets in those places, many of them beggars, that I did not stick out or attract the attention of the authorities. I never begged for money off passers-by, which also helped to keep me out of trouble with the authorities. I could not have brought myself to do that. I did not see myself as a beggar, just as a child who had somehow got stranded and needed to find a way to move forward with his life and get himself an education.

In the end I decided to sleep among the rocks beneath the legs of a flyover (later I would learn it's the one close to the Ellis Park stadium), with traffic roaring past on both sides. It was hard to rest with the threatening noises of the night-time city all around. I was quite scared but I got through the night. In the morning I was able to wash in the bathroom of a petrol station down the road. Then I walked up a main road until I saw the Cathedral of Christ the King, the Catholic Archdiocese in Johannesburg. Its steps and doors were protected by high walls but the gates stood open.

There was a priest inside who knew the Combonis' telephone number and agreed to make a call for me. I was lucky that he got through to Father Albino Adot. The priest told Father Albino that I had now arrived in South Africa and was desperate for a place to stay.

Father Albino said that he had to get permission from his superiors before he could agree to take me in. He gave the priest a number for the head of the Comboni Missionaries, Father Giuseppe (Joe) Sandri. I called the number later that day and to my surprise Father Sandri answered the phone himself.

'I'm afraid we have no space,' he said, although his voice sounded kind and genuinely regretful.

I became quite despondent, not knowing who else I could turn to. If the Combonis couldn't help me, where would I go next?

The priest at the cathedral, who also told me that they had nowhere for me to sleep, had given me a few rands, so I went to a phone shop from where I could call the Combonis again. I gave the woman my last R10 and just kept ringing the mission, begging for work and for somewhere to sleep, telling whoever I got on the phone how far I had travelled and how I had spent the night under the flyover. Everyone I spoke to listened politely but they were all adamant: there was no room for me.

Eventually I admitted defeat and gave up, dropping the phone back onto the receiver. As I turned to leave the phone shop the woman called me back. 'You have spent R25 on calls,' she told me. 'You need to pay me for the difference.'

'I don't have any more money,' I admitted.

'Then I am calling the police,' she told me.

'Oh no,' I thought, 'not prison and deportation again!'

Despair and tiredness overwhelmed me and I started to cry. Standing in front of the woman I sobbed uncontrollably and she must have felt pity for me.

'Okay, okay,' she said. 'Stop crying. You don't have to pay.'

I made my way back to the cathedral to beg the priest one more time to find a corner of the great building for me to sleep, but he remained as adamant as the Combonis: there was nowhere for me to lay my head. Today I realise that the priest must have received many such requests on a daily basis, as many African immigrants flocked to the Johannesburg city centre when the country's borders opened to them after the first democratic elections. He knew that if he allowed me to stay just one night, he might become responsible for me for many weeks or months.

I told him how scared I was the previous night sleeping under the flyover. 'If there is nowhere for me inside, may I sleep outside on the cathedral steps?' I pleaded.

He looked at me for a while and sighed deeply. 'Let me phone Father Sandri again,' he said.

'I have this 17-year-old boy here,' I heard him telling the Father, 'with nowhere to go, and he is planning to sleep on the steps outside the cathedral. The only people he knows in the city are you people. What can I do with him?'

He listened for a few moments, thanked Father Sandri and hung up the phone.

'He says he will come and pick you up,' he told me and I went back outside to wait in the shade on one of the benches.

At about six in the evening, a white Mazda 323 turned in

through the gates of the cathedral and a friendly-looking man with grey hair, glasses and moustache bounced out of the driver's seat.

'Where is the boy?' Father Sandri asked the priest, letting out a chuckle that I was soon to learn was part of his normal way of speaking.

'Here,' I said.

'Okay,' he said, 'come with me. Where are your belongings?'

'I don't have any.'

I was struck by how calm and cheerful he was, and I would soon discover that he was always like this. I never saw him get angry. Whenever a crisis arose he would always laugh and make a joke and then deal with the problem later. It was a good lesson for a naturally impulsive and impatient person like me to learn. Little did I know, as I drove away with him that evening, that I would learn a great deal more from Father Sandri in the coming years.

Father Sandri drove me to the headquarters of the Combonis, which was a big house sitting behind high electric gates in the hilly residential area of Kensington, a suburb east of the city centre. As the gates swung open and we drove in, it felt like entering a private paradise. There were vines along the short drive, heavy with grapes, and a neatly tended lawn below the parking area. Broad steps swept up to the front door.

Inside, we walked through the entrance hall and into a room at the back of the house. Light flooded in from a wall of glass, revealing a panoramic view of the city below. Father Sandri introduced me to another Italian, Father Enrico Radaelli, and a dynamic Italian/German called Brother Peter Niederbrunner.

They showed me where to shower and where I would sleep, in a very pleasant annex over the garages that had been turned into a dormitory with bunk beds.

Then they sat me down and asked me lots of questions about where I had come from. I found myself answering with more honesty and more detail than I usually found comfortable. Something about them made me feel safe. It was as if I had finally come home.

After my shower, of course, I had to put on the same filthy clothes I had been travelling in for so long. The Brothers fed me and then I went to my bunk and fell into a deep sleep. Brother Peter came knocking on my door at six the following morning to get me up for prayers in the small chapel that had been created in a room beside the front door.

After Mass we had breakfast and I ate at least three bread rolls, my body perhaps trying to make up for the malnourishment of the past few months. That day Brother Peter went to the shops and bought me some clothes and underwear, a gesture of consideration and kindness I'd never received before from anyone but my mother.

They suggested that I work in their garden in exchange for my bed and board. I was more than happy to accept the offer, willing to work from the moment I woke to the moment I went to bed, only taking breaks when summoned in for meals and prayers. I was willing to do anything I could to make them want to keep me there.

What I liked about Brother Peter was that, like me, he always ran everywhere. When he gave me a job in the garden, he would always come out and work alongside me. In the following months we built walls down each side of the garden to raise beds for vegetables, and when we loaded up the truck with rubbish to go to the dump he would drive with me sitting beside him and would help me unload it as if it was the most natural thing in the world. I noticed that when most white South Africans drove to the rubbish dump with a black person, they would make the black person sit in the back with the rubbish and would not get out to help them unload.

We always worked together, washed together and ate together, and he gradually revealed his past to me. Born on a farm in South Tyrol, a German-speaking area of northern Italy, Peter was the youngest of 11 children and had to start working on a neighbour's farm at the age of nine. It surprised me to hear that some people in Europe are poor, just like people in Africa, but that they work hard to overcome those hardships. In Africa we are born into hardship; we never learn from it, but rather blame others for our suffering. By doing so we accept the status of permanent victims, with no control over our destiny. We remain forever dependent, despite living on a rich continent. If only Africans would take responsibility for their failure, then we would get out of our current predicament.

The Comboni missionaries invited me into their midst even though they didn't know anything about me beyond what I had told them. For all they knew I could have been a killer on the run, but they chose to believe my story. It seemed as if my life was finally changing for the better and I felt a warm glow of happiness in my heart as my self-esteem started to rise. There were peach trees in the garden, and one day Brother Peter even allowed me to help him make jam with the fruit. It truly felt like I had arrived in paradise.

With the dog Jambo at the Combonis' house in Johannesburg

There was a field running steeply down the hill below the garden, which also belonged to the priests but had been neglected and was now a tangle of weeds, some of them large saplings. It had not been looked after for a long time, so once I had got the front garden into shape, I offered to set about cleaning the field up for them. I did a beautiful job, but the weeds were tenacious and I ended up with deep cuts all over my hands at the end of each day.

After that I drained and washed the swimming pool, which stood below the windows of the main room, overlooking the city-scape, getting painful acid burns in the open cuts on my palms. But I didn't care about any of these wounds as long as they allowed me to stay. I was learning so much from them, from the simplest things, such as how to eat with cutlery instead of using my hands, to abstract political and philosophical ideas. They talked to me as if I was their educational equal and their friend.

Once I'd cleaned up the garden, I didn't have much to do, so I set about finding other sources of income. I was happy to try my hand at any sort of work. I even tried labouring on a building site, but after a week of intense physical pain I realised that I was not built to spend my days carrying cement up ladders and flights of stairs on my head, working ten hours a day for a few rands. I managed to get some gardening jobs at houses in the neigh-bourhood and I was always meticulous and conscientious in my work.

I also persuaded the owner of a tile shop to give me a job. I helped him load tiles into his truck and he paid me R50 a day, which seemed like quite a lot of money. There was another worker in the tile shop who came from Natal, called Daniel. He couldn't read or write and I was able to teach him how to sign his name.

One day Daniel didn't turn up for work. I went to the hostel where I knew he was staying, all set to tell him off for leaving me on my own. Other residents there told me that the previous night Daniel had been drinking with friends and had been accused by a drunk of making eye contact with his girlfriend. Without any provocation the other man had pulled out a knife and stabbed

Daniel to death. His body was now lying in the mortuary and there was no way of contacting his family since they had no phone and no one knew their physical address.

This incident reminded me that if the same thing happened to me, my family would also never find out my fate. The Combonis had trusted that I was telling them the truth about my roots and had no idea who my family were or how to find them in an emergency. Just like Daniel, I had never been able to call my mother since leaving the country because she had no access to a telephone, and I hadn't been able to write to her because her house had no number and her street had no name. She was just one more anonymous person living in a mud hut. I had no idea what might have happened to her, or to my brothers and sisters, during my travels. For all I knew she might already be dead. It occurred to me that she might well be thinking the same about me.

Daniel's death left me traumatised for several days.

Early in December the Fathers had a meeting about what to do with me and called me in to hear what they had decided. Remembering what had happened at the family meeting in Kenya, I entered the room in trepidation.

'You are a very good worker,' Father Enrico told me. 'We would like to help you find a place to stay in the new year. We will pay half the rent. You will work for us two days a week and you can find a job somewhere else for the rest of the week.'

'Please,' I said, 'I want to go to school.'

'How are you going to do that?' he asked. 'Do you have any certificates?'

'No,' I admitted. 'Nothing.'

'So how are you going to prove to the teachers that you have been to school before?'

'If you show me a school book,' I said, 'I'll show you what I can do.'

They went away to talk about it further, and then Father Enrico came back. 'I'm sorry,' he said, 'there is no money for schooling. We can't help.'

He suddenly seemed to be very harsh when he talked, and I felt that now he didn't like me for some reason, that he saw me as a burden in the same way my mother's family had. Perhaps he thought I was abusing their generosity and asking too much.

The meeting left me anxious, and I felt I needed to do everything perfectly around the house. About a week later I was washing Brother Peter's car, and I dropped the cloth on the ground and picked it up without rinsing the grit out, making a big scratch in the paintwork. Brother Peter was so furious that I think he would have beaten me and thrown me out there and then if Father Sandri hadn't come to my rescue and calmed the situation down with his usual good humour.

However, Brother Peter also showed me more kindness than anyone I had ever met before. When we celebrated Christmas, he bought me some chocolate and a card that played a tune when you opened it. It was the first Christmas present I had received, apart from the clothes that my mother would buy us when we were tiny, or the biscuits that neighbours might give us when we knocked on their doors in the village to wish them a happy Christmas.

I was overwhelmed by the whole Christmas experience with the Combonis. I helped Brother Peter put up a tree, and for the first time I felt I had a real father, someone I could trust, someone who would advise me when I was doing things wrong and reward me when I did something good. I knew, however, that he was unsure if they could afford to keep helping me in the long term, and that worried me.

Shortly after I arrived at the Combonis, Father Enrico also took me to apply for refugee status at the Department of Home Affairs in Germiston so that I would at least have the required documentation to remain in the country legally.

When I was born, my mother gave me the birth names Emmanuel Malish Taban. 'Malish' means 'apology', which was her way of saying sorry for what she put me through during her pregnancy, when things were bad between her and my father, who had even beaten her up at times. 'Taban' means 'suffering'. When I applied for refugee status, I decided to create a new identity by not taking my father's surname, and not giving my uncles on my mother's side any further say in my life by using her surname. Instead, I started my own family tree by using my third birth name as a surname.

From my first days at the Combonis, I kept pestering them about wanting to return to school, no doubt driving them mad with my stubbornness. In January 1996 Father Sandri spoke to Father Joseph Ukelo, the other South Sudanese priest now based in South Africa. Father Ukelo was working at a Catholic church in a village called Nhlazatshe, close to Badplaas (now eManzana) in Mpumalanga. He suggested that I try to get into Chief Jerry Nkosi Secondary School in a small village nearby.

I jumped at the offer and was accepted by the school.

Father Sandri bought me another change of clothes and some groceries and we drove in his white Mazda to a house in a compound beside the Catholic church in Nhlazatshe, which was about 240 kilometres from Johannesburg. Apart from Father Ukelo, a Mexican priest lived in the house. There was a spare room for me.

'You can stay here,' Father Sandri told me, 'and the school is just a few kilometres down the road. We will give you R50 every month to help you buy soap and any other basic supplies that you need.'

Father Ukelo was a big man who liked to cook himself giant portions of rice and chicken, which he would eat while watching boxing on television, cheering on his favourite fighters. I enjoyed staying with the two priests and it was great being able to speak to a fellow countryman again and to share memories of Sudan. However, I was ashamed of some of the things that had happened to me in the past two years, for instance that I had spent time in prison, so I didn't tell him too much about myself.

When I first arrived at Chief Jerry Nkosi Secondary School, the headmaster told me I would be in Standard Eight (Grade 10), which meant I could complete high school in three years. But I had already seen the maths textbook and thought that I should be in Standard Nine (Grade 11), even though I had only had about five years of schooling in Sudan. I somehow managed to convince him that I should be placed in Standard Nine.

Although many of the classes at Chief Jerry Nkosi were taught in English, most people spoke Swazi, the local language. However, the teachers insisted that every learner should communicate in

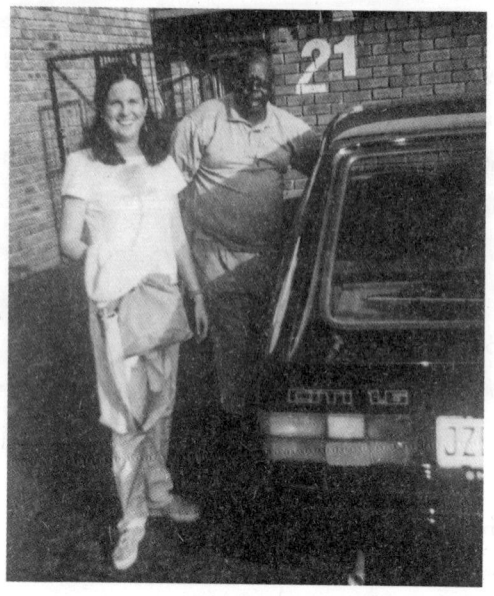

Father Joseph Ukelo with a friend who came to visit

English in the classes that I attended, so that I wouldn't be excluded. None of my fellow classmates objected to this inconvenience, making me feel very welcome in their community.

Once again, I enjoyed my classes, especially maths and science. In English, however, I struggled, and then they told me I needed to do a second language as well. I chose Afrikaans. It was an unusual choice for a boy like me, and the teachers were impressed that I was willing to try. One of them even offered to give me extra lessons in her home for free, often feeding me while I was with her as well. Her name was Mahlaba, but I called her 'Mistress' or 'Mama' and came to think of her with great respect. She had a nice house very close to the school. It felt like an honour to be invited into someone's family home and I always made sure I was punctual

126

for my lessons. She became a good friend and I owe a great deal to her, and to the other kind, wise people who decided to help me along the way.

Sometimes my grasp of English would let me down while I was studying. I would become frustrated because I could not understand the full meaning of the book I was reading. When that happened, I would keep reading the same pages over and over again, even if it took me until three in the morning, until I understood what was being explained. I refused to accept that there was anything I could not understand if I worked hard enough at it. If other people could do it, I reasoned, then there was no reason why I shouldn't be able to do it too.

We soon discovered that taking the bus to and from school every day was too expensive, and so the brothers bought me a bicycle. The route was about 14 kilometres and I was happy to ride back and forth over the rough dirt roads of the settlements, especially when I could cruise down the steep hills without pedalling, enjoying the views that stretched away in every direction. But it meant that I arrived at school covered in mud and dust, not to mention being bathed in my own sweat. I would always try to travel at full speed, as I had done all my life, when it probably would have been more sensible to go at a steady pace and conserve my energy, particularly on hot summer days.

There was also a long and steep hill that I had to cycle back up at the end of each school day. An elderly German priest, who lived along the route and was part of the Comboni mission, noticed me toiling past his house each day and made sure he was always waiting outside with a drink of water and a sandwich for me, so that

I could break my journey. As winter arrived the problem became the cold rather than the heat, and sometimes even snow, something I had not encountered before.

At the bottom of the hill, close to the school, there was a river that swelled dangerously when the rains came. On those days I would have to wait for the water to subside before I could cross, making me frustratingly late for class. Sometimes, if I was lucky, a passing truck driver would take pity on me and give the bicycle and me a lift through the torrent. I only once missed a day of school due to bad weather.

I cycled back and forth each day for about four months before everyone decided it was too much and they moved me into an abandoned priest's house right next to the school. Opposite was an eating house, which was always emitting loud music and voices. The Combonis gave me another package of groceries and R150 a month to look after myself.

At first I was able to eat well, and I was even able to feed some of the new friends I was making, many of whom were just as poor as me. Once those groceries had run out, however, the money that the Comboni missionaries were giving me each month was no longer really enough to live on comfortably. I was so determined not to drop out of school now that I had finally managed to get my education started again, however, that I subsisted on a diet of beans and not much else. I also had to stop handing my food around quite so freely.

During my two years at Chief Jerry Nkosi I also had to renew my refugee status every three months in Johannesburg, which meant a taxi trip to the city on Sunday and a return trip on Tuesday. The Refugee Centre was a very rough place and one

In the Johannesburg CBD on one of the many trips to renew my refugee status

of the priests would always come with me, because being with a white man helped to speed things along. Even so, to get seen you had to get up at three in the morning in order to get a place in the queue and you probably wouldn't reach the front of that queue until about three in the afternoon. I very much resented the amount of study time I was wasting on such bureaucracy, but anything was better than being deported or thrown back into jail.

Almost the moment I arrived at Chief Jerry Nkosi I made friends with a boy called David Zulu, whose family lived just up the road. We often played soccer after school on the field beside the elementary school opposite his house, but I would nearly always be the first to leave the games because I wanted to get back to my books at home. David hadn't been treating school very seriously until he met me, but we pushed each other to study hard and as a result he passed the exams well.

9 A SINGLE-MINDED STUDENT

I worked very hard at my lessons and was determined not to waste a single second of school time because I never knew when my education was going to be cut short again. By the time I came to sit my final matric exams at the end of 1997, I was one of the top candidates in the area, scoring 57 per cent, and was awarded an exemption to go to university even though I didn't yet know what I wanted to study.

People had told me that I would make the most money if I became an actuary or went into engineering. My friend David, who also passed his exams with exemptions, was accepted to study for a Bachelor of Science degree at the University of the Free State, but due to lack of funds he could not start immediately. When I went back to Johannesburg and Father Sandri asked me what I wanted to do, I knew I needed to make a decision. So I told him, 'Engineering'.

'Okay,' he said, 'see if you can get a place at Wits University and we will try to help you get there.'

In January 1998, when I was queuing to register at the university, I noticed that the girl in front of me had scored 78 per cent in her exams. I realised I might be in trouble with my 57 per cent. We got talking and she suggested that if I couldn't get into engineering, I should apply for accounting. Sure enough, when I got to the front of the queue, they informed me that my marks were too low.

'How about medicine?' I asked.

'It is closed, sorry.'

Remembering the advice of the girl in the queue, I went to the accounting department and saw that there were queues around the block.

'How many people are trying to get in here?' I asked.

'About 3 000,' I was informed.

That did not sound like good odds to me either. I had heard about Wits technical college (Technikon Witwatersrand), so I walked over to it and was told I would be accepted to study electrical engineering. At first I was very excited to actually be offered anything, but then I felt some doubts creeping in.

'Why are you willing to accept me if Wits University weren't?' I asked.

'Because here it is technical and at Wits University it is theoretical. There's a big difference.'

'But which one is better?' I asked.

'Obviously it is better to study at university because then you can design stuff.'

Disappointed, I gathered up my forms and returned to the Comboni headquarters to rethink my position.

'Did you find a university?' Father Sandri asked as I sat down with him and Brother Peter.

'No,' I lied, 'I want to repeat my matric.'

'If you repeat matric,' Brother Peter said, 'where are you going to stay? We have nowhere for you. We have supported you for over two years and now you need to find work.'

'No,' Father Sandri came to my defence yet again, 'it's okay. You go and find a school.'

I went to see the headmaster at a nearby school, but he told me they couldn't help me improve on the marks I already had. I then went to Jeppe High School for Boys, where the deputy headmaster, an Irishman called Teacher Ross, told me that he thought they would be able to improve on my marks and offered me a place in his 'A' class.

This school was very different from the haphazard collection of buildings that made up Chief Jerry Nkosi. These grand old buildings, surrounded by expensive houses and well-maintained roads, looked like the sort of schools in Europe and America that I had seen pictures of. The children coming and going through the gates all looked smart in their uniforms, as if they came from prosperous families, although I'm sure there were many like me who had struggled to be there.

When Brother Peter, who was responsible for the finances of the mission, heard that the school fees were about R12 000 for the year, he nearly exploded, saying that they couldn't afford to spend so much money on one person. I felt terrible about having to ask for yet more charity, but eventually he relented and went to pay the fees.

However, when he returned from the school that day, Brother Peter told me that Jeppe was willing to give me a scholarship so that I could study for free. All I needed to buy in order to attend was a school blazer. He must've told them my story of how I ended up

Father (later Bishop) Joe Sandri who became like a father to me

in South Africa. I have never felt so relieved. I saw it as a sign that someone in authority actually believed in me and my potential and were willing to back that belief up with a generous financial offer.

Brother Peter bought me the blazer and Father Sandri also gave me a black briefcase that had belonged to a bishop who had passed on. I was ready to get back to work once more. To help with buying the clothes and food that I needed, I worked for a local shopkeeper during the holidays.

Walking in a week or two after the official start of the school year, I made friends with a boy called Siyabonga Mkhize. His family lived in one of the nearby houses and I found it very encouraging to think that it was possible for black people to live in such nice places. He was about six years younger than me. His father had risen to be a bank manager, but Siyabonga was struggling with his maths and I was able to help him.

'One day,' I told myself when he first took me home to meet his family, 'I will be able to live in a house like this in an area like this.'

There were 24 of us in 'A' class: me and another black guy called Jimmy, two Indians and the rest were white guys. Even though the apartheid system was gone, there was still a huge gulf between white and black in South Africa in 1998. Jimmy was always very supportive: for instance, when the white guys told me that I had a weird accent, he stood up for me and told them that it was their problem, not mine.

While I got along with the white boys in class I could never socialise with them, even when they invited me. I was ashamed of my poverty and made up a story that my father was the vice president of South Sudan. I was embarrassed by who I really was and how lowly my beginnings had been. Some of the boys from school drove past the Combonis' house one day and saw me sweeping the pavement outside. They even reversed to confirm what they had seen, and were obviously shocked. They thought I was from a wealthy family and hadn't expected to find me working for my pocket money. None of them, however, ever challenged me on it, and I was grateful for that.

Halfway through the first term the headmaster singled me out for a performance award of R500. He wanted me to tell my life story to the school as an inspiration at the awards ceremony, but

I didn't want everyone to know how poor I was, so I stayed away that day and got my award the following morning.

During that year I applied for an actuarial science course and was accepted, but I was not sure that it was what I wanted to do. I guess I was influenced by my classmates, since nearly all of them wanted to do accounting. Engineering and medicine were my other choices but I was rejected for both of them.

Then Diana Beamish, a former nun whom I had first met at the Refugee Centre and who had started an organisation for refugees called Mercy House in 1994, told me about the Japan International Volunteer Centre, which was sponsoring people to study health care. I applied and they agreed to support me. In November I therefore applied to study medicine at the University of Pretoria (UP), the University of the Witwatersrand and the Medical University of South Africa (Medunsa, today the Sefako Makgatho Health Sciences University), a tertiary institution originally built exclusively for black students during apartheid. UP and Wits put me on their waiting lists, which meant my chances of getting in were very slim.

I passed my final exams well this time, even gaining a distinction, and the Japan International Volunteer Centre agreed to pay for all my tuition and even some of my accommodation costs. The Combonis also gave me a little more money to help with my living expenses. I was elated when Medunsa informed me in January 1999 that they could accommodate me.

On my first day at the Medunsa campus in Ga-Rankuwa, northwest of Pretoria, I was beaming. Here I was, starting out on my journey to become a doctor. I couldn't help but think of my mother and wondered what she would say if she could see me. Because my mother had no telephone I had not been able to contact her since the day I left South Sudan.

In the first year of medical studies you're studying basic science. One of our most important subjects, which I found quite difficult, was chemistry. The first time I went to the chemistry lab to find a place, I was joined by a fellow student who introduced himself as Rodney Mudau. He was from Venda. He told me he had picked me out because I had been asking a lot of questions during the introductory sessions. However, I soon found out he actually wanted to be in my group because he hoped I would introduce him to one of the girls he had seen me talking to. Unfortunately, the girl rejected him, but Rodney and I still became good friends.

We befriended a girl called Salome Dlangamandla from Lesotho and the three of us studied hard together, all of us being very competitive. We became a tight group of three and Rodney became like a brother to me, despite the fact that he was shy and had difficulty relating to people. When I got married some years later, he was my best man, by which time he was a highly qualified neurologist.

I realised in my first year that university life exposes you to people from different backgrounds and interests. In many ways the decisions you make with regard to friendships influence whether you will excel in your studies. I was lucky that I fell in with Rodney and Salome, who were very focused, and not with some partying crowd.

With my university friends Mfundo   *My friends spoiled me with a huge*
Makhubela (left) and Rodney Mudau (right)   *cake on my 24th birthday*

One first-year course that I learned much from was in psychology. Previously, I had relied on religion to explain many things about the human condition, but psychology helped me to understand things differently. It taught me that in certain circumstances people start to accept the conditions they are subjected to. It made me realise that many of my fellow countrymen had subconsciously taken on an attitude of helplessness and victimhood.

Being a foreigner and having a darker skin made me an outsider among many of the other students, so I concentrated all my time on studying alone or with Rodney and Salome. There were students who would tease me that I was a devil because of my colour. There was one particular girl who I got on well with and wanted to date. I asked her friend to find out if I had a chance. She came back to tell me that her friend really liked me and that she would have gone out with me if only my skin had been lighter. She suggested I should use some creams to try to lighten my complexion. I didn't understand that mentality at all.

In 2000, my second year, I was allocated to share room 210 in block 5B with Tumi Makweya, who would later become famous as the gospel singer Dr Tumi. We got on well but he, like virtually everyone else on campus, would go home during the holidays, leaving me on my own. I would spend a lot of my time walking around the university grounds, sometimes just stopping to stare at the cars passing by on the roads outside the fences, imagining that one day it would be me speeding by in a shiny new BMW or Mercedes.

It was on one of these quiet weekends during the Easter holidays, when I was studying in my room, that there was a knock on my door at about four in the afternoon. When I opened it slightly I found a man in his twenties and a boy of about 12 outside.

'I'm looking for your roommate,' the man said.

'He's not around,' I replied, 'he's at home.'

'Can I leave him a message?' He asked.

Because he was with a young boy I thought he must be okay so I opened the door wider to let them in while I looked for a pen and paper. As I turned away he brought the butt of his gun down on the back of my head, knocking me to the floor. He pushed the barrel into my face and ordered me to lie still.

'Don't scream,' he hissed.

Scooping up my phone, my computer, my wallet and anything else he could find, including my food, he demanded to know my bank PIN number. I had the presence of mind to give him the wrong number and to repeat the same number when he asked me again a few minutes later. The two of them then ran off, locking the door behind them and taking the key.

Once the sound of their running feet had faded away, I was left with nothing but silence. I tried shouting for help, but there was no response. I opened the window because normally there were students walking across the grass below on their way to the cafeteria, but that day there was no one. After a few hours, as it grew dark, I started to feel hungry and I realised it could be two or three days before Tumi or anyone else came back to release me.

The room was on the second floor and if I had tried to jump I would undoubtedly have broken my legs – or worse. There was a narrow ledge, probably less than a metre wide, which ran along below the windows. If I could crawl along there, I decided, tapping on windows as I went, I might eventually find someone who could let me in. The only problem was my fear of heights.

I tried shouting for a little longer, but no one responded. There didn't seem to be any option.

I inched my way out through the narrow opening of the window onto the ledge head-first, being careful not to look down, and made my way to the first window. There was no one there. The same empty rooms greeted me all the way along the building until the final one, where a fellow student had managed to smuggle his girlfriend in for a little private time. It was embarrassing but I had no option but to tap on the window, which frightened them both half to death. Luckily they recognised me and let me in once they realised what had happened. It was such a relief to be safely back on solid ground.

The campus security guards were very sympathetic but there was little they could do about the incident. I learned that it was not the first time such a thing had happened. The university was surrounded by townships where people with nothing to lose could see students through the fences, going about their lives. We must have looked like easy pickings, with our phones and computers and frequent visits to cash machines.

I couldn't believe that I had lost all my possessions again, just like I had so many times before on my journey from Sudan to South Africa. None of my friends were there for me to talk to, and because I had lost my cellphone I couldn't call anyone. I used my last few rands to buy myself a box of the wine that I had some-times seen the Combonis sipping. I then proceeded to drown my sorrows, not stopping until I was vomiting like never before.

By the time Tumi came back a day later, the room smelled like hell and I realised I did not have a single penny left in the world. I had to wash all my clothes and bedding and felt so low and mis-erable I vowed never to allow myself to get that drunk again. One positive outcome was that after the incident, the university author-ities allowed me to move to a room of my own, where I stayed until I graduated, able to study in peace.

I became very antisocial when I was studying, not wanting the distraction of other people, and I would use music to inspire me.

The avid student on his way to the library at Medunsa

I was wary of making any friends unless I knew they would be the sort of people to encourage me to study, like Rodney and Salome. I couldn't afford to lose focus because I felt I had already lost too many years. Studying and achieving good results made me happier than anything else, and I didn't want to be made to feel guilty for not returning people's calls or for turning down social invitations that I knew would cut into my studying time. It was easier just to keep myself to myself.

Of course, in our second year we also took classes in anatomy. Despite my experiences as a child I found it rather disconcerting seeing all those dead people. After my first anatomy class I was quite nauseous and upset, but I told myself I wasn't going to chicken out.

In June of my second year at Medunsa, I received a letter to say that the South African government had forbidden the Japan International Volunteer Centre from sponsoring foreigners, so they were going to terminate my scholarship. My study fees were paid up to the end of that year, but I would receive my allowance only for three more months. How, I wondered, could I continue without the money to eat and buy books?

A few months before, Father Sandri had been appointed secretary-general of the Comboni Missionaries and had to move to their international headquarters in Rome. I therefore had to turn to Brother Peter and the other priests at the mission in Johannesburg to find out how I was going to pay my fees in the future. They seemed quite calm about it, assuring me that something would turn up, just as it always had in the past.

A few weeks later I went to the Comboni house on a Friday to help with the garden and to stay the weekend, as I had to renew my papers at the Refugee Centre that Monday. At that time, I also met the priest who had replaced Father Sandri. I was lucky, as I got my papers renewed by midday on Monday, after which I took a taxi back to the Comboni house and then left for the Medunsa campus in Pretoria by taxi.

Not long after I got back to my room, there was a knock on my door. When I opened it, there stood Brother Peter and Father Enrico. They told me that the priest who had replaced Father Sandri had lost a gun and a watch, and believed I had taken them. He had instructed them to search my belongings. I was shocked beyond belief. I had not been accused of stealing anything since I was a young boy living with my uncle. I did not protest because I had nothing to hide, and of course they found nothing in my room.

The Father, however, insisted that it must have been me who stole his possessions. I was informed that I was no longer welcome at the Comboni house. Having cut myself adrift from my mother, I had found great comfort in being part of the Comboni community and had looked on them as my replacement family. I was devastated, and I felt I had lost my home all over again and had no one else to turn to in my hour of need.

The only person I could turn to was Simon Donnelly, a lecturer in the department of linguistics at the University of the Witwatersrand, whom I had met through Diana Beamish. Diana, who was Simon's godmother, had asked him to help me with my Afrikaans when I was at Jeppe High. As a student, he would often take me to the movies on a Friday evening, because he knew I didn't have the money to go on my own, and sometimes he would buy me a pizza afterwards. When I had to go into Johannesburg to renew my documents, I would now stay with Simon.

At this time, when my finances looked at their most precarious, I developed a hernia, which required surgery. Unfortunately the wound went septic and I had to stay in the Ga-Rankuwa

Hospital (today the Dr George Mukhari Academic Hospital) on campus for ten days. I felt very alone in the ward when I saw all the other patients with their families coming in bearing fruit and gifts, reminding me that none of my family knew I was there. Rodney and Salome, my two faithful friends, were the only ones who came to visit me.

Brother Peter sent me a little bit of money to keep me afloat, but he didn't come to see me and I felt very hurt. The consultant would come on his rounds with my classmates, discuss me as a medical case and then move on without doing anything.

One of the nurses must have seen how alone I was and felt sorry for me. She took the time to ask me about my family, and she was the first person I ever told my whole story to. After I was discharged she invited me to come to her house every day so that she could dress my wound, because it was still oozing pus. After a week of visiting her she found that the surgeon had left a suture in the wound. She removed it and I immediately healed.

When the university closed for the December holidays at the end of 2000 I had nowhere to go. I was no longer welcome at the Combonis and it wasn't an option to stay with Simon. At the time Father Albino Adot, one of the South Sudanese Comboni priests based in South Africa, was working at the Glen Cowie Catholic Mission in a rural part of Limpopo province. There was a hospital called St Rita's at the mission, and through Father Albino I asked the superintendent whether I could do an elective there during the holidays. To my relief, he agreed to let me work there in exchange for accommodation and food.

Without the scholarship, money became even more of a worry

Brother Peter Niederbrunner has taught me many valuable life lessons and supported me on my journey. Here we are at Wits University in 2018, when I graduated as a pulmonologist.

in my third year than it had been before. Thankfully, I had learned a very important lesson from Brother Peter early on. He advised me that whenever I received any sum of money, even for a bursary or sponsorship, I should always try to save half of it. I didn't have much but at least I wasn't penniless, as I had been for most of my journey to South Africa.

I knew from my childhood and teenage years that I could survive on very little food, and I believed that with willpower I could, to a large extent, overcome the need for regular meals. After all, during my travels I had sometimes gone several days without eating and I had survived. So, to stretch what little I had as far as I possibly could once university restarted, I took to eating only once a day, in the evening. I was also forced to think up all sorts of ways to dodge my friends when they invited me to do anything that might involve spending cash. I would pass the lunch hours out of sight in the library and I gradually became more and more isolated socially.

At the same time I was feeling insecure about my temporary refugee status, aware that at any stage the authorities could arbitrarily refuse to renew my permit, just as they had stopped the Japan International Volunteer Centre from continuing to pay for my scholarship, and I would be sent packing. However, as worried as I was, I was still determined to keep my education going for as long as I possibly could. It now felt like it was the only thing I had left in life.

It was hard to keep awake and to concentrate when I was always hungry. Twice I collapsed while we were doing practicals in the hospital because I was hypoglycaemic, but I kept getting back up and continuing the struggle from day to day. One of the women working in the university cafeteria must have guessed how poor and hungry I was, because when I went to the canteen for my food in the evenings, she would give me extra-large helpings. That way I was able to go back to my room, eat half and keep the other half for the next day. It was a matter of surviving from one day to the next.

The important thing for me was always to keep studying, and I had never found the reading part of that difficult. Writing essays was still a challenge for me, and however hard I tried it was difficult to get marks of more than 80 per cent. I found my own shortcomings with language incredibly frustrating.

Even though I was banished from the Comboni house, neither Brother Peter nor Bishop Sandri had completely given up on me. When Bishop Sandri heard about my predicament, he sent some money from Italy, and all the while Brother Peter was looking for sponsors for my third year. He also sent me small amounts for food and pocket money without telling his superiors.

Franz Pahl, a well-known politician in South Tyrol, an autonomous region in northern Italy, had grown up in the same village

Franz Pahl

as Brother Peter. Sometime during my third year, Franz visited South Africa and stayed with Brother Peter, who told him my story. Franz kindly offered to sponsor not only my third year but also the remainder of my medical studies.

Franz didn't have any children of his own and he also sponsored refugees from Eastern Europe. He would regularly make contact with me via email, and later Skype, always interested to know more about my life and my studies. Thanks to his wonderful sense of humour and his interest, we developed a great rapport and so started a friendship that continues to this day.

In the middle of 2001, something changed at the Combonis. I was later told that one of the domestic workers at the house had found the missing watch. Shortly afterwards, the Father who had accused me of stealing it was voted out from his position and was replaced by a kindly Italian priest. I was allowed to return to the place that had been my home from home. Many years later, Brother Peter told me how bad he and Father Enrico had felt about the accusations of theft that were levelled against me, because they had not believed for a moment that I was guilty.

I was very relieved and also proud that I had not given up on myself or my dreams of getting an education when everything had looked so hopeless. I learned many valuable lessons about life and about people during that time, and I also started to be much more careful with money, striving always to have some saved in case things went wrong again.

10 BECOMING A DOCTOR

In 2002, during my fourth year of medical school, I decided it was time to get a driving licence and wrote my learner's exam. I had heard that the traffic officials in Johannesburg who performed the driver's licence test often insisted on a bribe, especially if you were a foreigner, and therefore decided to rather do the test in another province. I also still needed a car to practise in and to use for the actual test.

So I reached out to Professor Taban Lo Liyong, the Sudanese writer and public figure whom my mother had told me about as a young boy. At the time he was the head of the Centre for African Studies and the linguistics department at the University of Venda in Thohoyandou. I asked him whether, as a fellow South Sudanese, he would be willing to assist me. The Combonis offered to pay him a small fee towards my accommodation, and that is how I ended up staying at his house practising my driving for three weeks. He, his wife and his daughters were all very hospitable and treated me like a member of the family.

I remember one day the professor took me to the nearby Kruger National Park and told me all about his life as we drove around, spotting the animals. Because he had always spoken out about the killing and raping of innocent villagers by SPLA soldiers, the rebel movement had never liked him.

In 2020, his outspoken political opinions about the consequences of the South Sudan states being reduced from 32 to 10, voiced in an open letter to a South Sudanese newspaper, cost him his job at the University of Juba. He was later reinstated after being fined three months' salary.

Considering how much he had achieved internationally, the professor had very little to show for it financially, which was an eye-opener for me. Because he was a famous thinker and public speaker, I assumed that he would live very differently from ordinary people. His openness and honesty helped me to see more clearly the truth of how the world works. It made me even more determined to establish myself in a career that would provide the sort of income our family needed in order for future generations to be lifted out of poverty once and for all.

Then I told him the whole story of my journey from our shared homeland to South Africa.

'One day,' he said, after I had finished, 'you should go back to southern Sudan and become a leader because you would be able to make a big difference.'

His compliment planted a seed. Imagine if I could go back one day and practise world-class medicine in a hospital in Sudan. Of course, at that point the country still had a long way to go before it could even afford to build such a facility. Meanwhile, I was still struggling to survive and progress in my own life, and new obstacles seemed to pop up every day.

In 2003, nine years after I had left my homeland, I saw an opportunity to make contact with my mother for the first time through Emeritus Bishop Paride Taban, who was on his way from Australia to South Sudan via Johannesburg and whom I had met at the Combonis' house. He was so happy to meet a fellow South Sudanese and was elated when he heard that I was studying to be a doctor. We spent some time together and he was happy to help me, even though he was a very important and busy person.

He promised to ask one of his colleagues in Sudan, Archbishop Paulino Lukudu, to look for my mother and, if she was still alive, to pass on a letter from me. I had no idea if the letter would ever reach her, but just writing it was exciting. I didn't go into detail about how hard my journey had been, but I told her that I was now in South Africa and studying to become a doctor.

Bishop Lukudu succeeded in tracking down my mother through her church and passed on my letter, which my sister Sarah then finally read to her. I have often tried to imagine what it must have felt like for her to hear the words of her son after grieving for me for all those years. Sarah told me that everyone in the house was crying as they listened and took in the enormity of what had happened to me since I had disappeared from their lives. Now that they knew I was alive, they wanted to talk to me as much as I wanted to talk to them.

Bishop Lukudu, who would later play a role in helping me establish a business in Sudan, arranged for my mother to get to a phone so that I could call. It was in June that I was able to hear her voice and the voices of my siblings again for the first time in so many years. It was a hard conversation; not having spoken Pojulu for so long, I had difficulty finding the right words and the right pronunciation. The gap between our lives was now so large, it was hard to think where to begin filling it in.

I learned that many things had changed since I had been away. My mother had trained to be a midwife in 1998, and the UN had provided her with a bicycle to get about. She had delivered more than 400 babies over the following years. She had also had another child herself. I now had a young sister called Beatrice. Of course my family had continued to evolve without me but now I wanted to rejoin them and do whatever I could to make our lives and futures better.

My mother was a remarkable woman and could have done so much more with her life if she had been luckier in her country of birth and choice of husband. Her education and prospects had been destroyed by unnecessary fighting, just as mine had been, and those of the generation after me. Imagine what a woman like that could have achieved if she had been given an education and had a supportive partner.

When I was a small child, she believed that I was the one who would benefit most from an education and did everything she could to make sure that I got one, despite the fact that she lived in a country torn apart by war and had no money and virtually no family support. Now she was weeping as she learned that not only was her lost son alive, when she had often assumed I was dead, but also that I was on the verge of becoming a doctor.

Many years later, Sarah told me that they had all been so certain I was dead that many in the family had wanted to give me the last rites, even though they had no body to bury, but Mom had refused, wanting to believe that I was still alive. There had been so many times during those years when I might have become just another anonymous body in the mortuary, it was easy to see why they all believed they would never see me again.

When my sponsor, Franz Pahl, heard that I had made contact again with my mother and the rest of my family, he sent me €5 000 to help my mother build a house. I sent the money on to my family, as I now had enough for my immediate needs at university. At last I had some money in the bank and could relax a little and socialise with fellow students – as long as it didn't interfere with my studies.

Lin-Lin

A few weeks before I made contact with my family, I met a young female student called Lin-Lin in a combined lecture group. She was originally from Myanmar (Burma) and was in her fourth year, while

I was in my fifth. Her father was a distinguished plastic surgeon, but Lin-Lin had been sent to South Africa to study due to the political unrest in her home country. Many of her family members were already working here as medical professionals.

She befriended me because she had noticed that I was the one who was always answering the questions and arguing with the lecturers in class. She seemed impressed by the amount of knowledge I had built up through my endless hours of reading and studying, and she liked to listen to me talk about everything that I had learned. It was not long before the friendship blossomed into love and she became my first proper girlfriend.

Because of her family background, Lin-Lin was much better off than me and drove around in a BMW. I didn't have a car, so she would drive me on our dates to movies and we would play music on the car stereo like other young lovers. Soon we moved in together. We were both very happy.

Lin-Lin listened when I talked about my dream of one day being able to return to Sudan. I told her how I wanted to build schools so that future generations of children could escape poverty as I had, and how I also wanted to do something about the corrupt system that had held the country back for so long.

Life was generally very good, although I was often reminded of my status as a foreigner. For one, when I applied for my internship early in 2004 I was told that the Department of Health didn't want to give me an internship because of my refugee status and the fact that my documents were usually only valid for three months, six at the most. This came as such a shock that it even impacted my performance at medical school. What would I do?

I couldn't qualify as a doctor without completing my internship.

When she heard the news, Diana Beamish wrote a letter to human rights lawyers, who then started to act on my behalf. They wrote to the Standing Committee for Refugee Affairs in the Department of Home Affairs, requesting that they grant me permission to apply for permanent residence so that I could complete my internship. The whole process cost me quite a bit of money, but thankfully I had received a bursary from the UN, which meant I could pay the lawyers' fees.

This whole process took around six months. It was only in November 2004 that I received the letter from the Standing Committee to say I could apply for permanent residence. I was very keen to do my internship at one of the hospitals in the Western Cape, but by that time all the positions had been allocated. I had to pick from the few positions that were still open, which is how I ended up at Kalafong Provincial Tertiary Hospital in Atteridgeville, Pretoria. I was placed only two weeks before I was supposed to start.

I finally graduated in December 2004 and it felt like the greatest achievement imaginable. Even though I received three distinctions during my exams, I only managed 47 per cent in my obstetrics final. The day before, I had been taken ill with what turned out to be a grumbling appendix. I was completely doped up on pethidine and struggled to answer even the easiest questions in the first part of the exam. After a few hours' sleep, however, I was able to score 100 per cent in the second part. The head of the department wanted to fail me because of the discrepancy between the two performances, which left me with an average of 53 per cent.

Graduating as medical doctor

Another problem was internal medicine. I scored 73 per cent when everyone else scored in the nineties because they had studied practice papers rather than reading the relevant books in their entirety, which was a short cut I refused to take. I wanted to have as thorough a knowledge as possible, not one based on simple exam revision, but that decision cost me the distinction that I had wanted so badly to obtain.

157

Guests at my graduation (from left to right): In front are Siyabonga Mkhize, Cynthia and Blessing Mkhize. At the back are Father John Converset, a friend, Professor Taban Lo Liyong, Lin-Lin, myself and Jenette Taban Lo Liyong.

In December 2004 I started working at Kalafong Hospital. I was supposed to do surgery (four months), internal medicine (four months), family medicine (two months) and paediatrics (two months). I started with surgery, and my first few days on call were in casualty. However, this was at the peak of the HIV/Aids pandemic in the country. The national antiretroviral therapy programme had been launched in April that year but had not yet made an impact.

I will never forget the sight of a hallway lined with stretchers, on which lay emaciated patients, many with diarrhoea. In places there were faeces on the floor. It was horrible to witness and made me doubt whether I had picked the right career. My colleagues who worked in internal medicine, and who were frequently called to casualty to treat patients, were exhausted.

This made me decide that internal medicine was perhaps not for me. I went back to the course coordinator and asked whether I could swap it for obstetrics and gynaecology, and so my rotation was changed.

On the first call I did in surgery I had to treat a woman who had deep vein thrombosis. As I tried to put in a drip, she moved around, and I got my first – and last – needle prick. I was immediately given antiretroviral treatment. When we tested the woman for HIV, it turned out that she had the virus. I was very relieved when I was tested later and had not contracted it.

Surgery brought other challenges too. I came up against a difficult and deeply prejudiced doctor, the consultant for the surgery department. He insisted on doing the ward rounds in Afrikaans, knowing that I wouldn't understand most of what he was saying, despite all the best efforts of my Afrikaans teachers. Even the registrar, who was English speaking, communicated in Afrikaans with the consultant and the students, many of whom were Afrikaans speakers.

Once I assisted the consultant in theatre when he was doing a hernia repair on the stomach of a white patient. I was busy holding back her stomach skin with an instrument when, the next moment, he told me to 'remove your dirty hands from the patient'. I was using an instrument and wearing gloves ...

When I was on call, he would also prefer to interact with white students rather than with me, a fellow doctor. When I insisted that he should deal with me as he would deal with a white colleague, he refused, so I started seeing patients without telling him. I made sure that I was as good as I could be at my work and that my patients were satisfied. It was during this time that I developed the habit of working for up to ten or twelve hours without drinking or eating anything. My only concern was the health of my patients and to learn how to be a good doctor.

Still, the consultant's attitude got to me. I gave up surgery when I had completed only two of the allotted four months. I left for obstetrics and gynaecology, feeling exhausted and angry, as this had been the first time I came up against such blatant racism.

Racism is a cunning force, though. It can find the weakness in anyone, even those who are emotionally strong. It takes only one weak moment to allow racism to consume you. But that proved to be the last time I would give in to the emotional weakness racism feeds on.

In the preceding months and especially after I started in obstetrics, I became aware that graduates of other universities looked down on those of us who had trained at Medunsa, a former black university. As part of our training as interns, we had to do a presentation to the registrar and the professor who was the head of obstetrics. I was asked to make a presentation about oral contraception.

I worked hard reading all the latest articles and research, but when I gave my talk the professor said he didn't agree with my findings. It was like he disapproved of me on principle. Because I have never been someone to take criticism without proper motivation, I showed him all the source materials I had used and he grudgingly agreed I was right. Soon I gained a reputation for being outspoken and for sticking up for myself and others if I thought we were being treated unfairly.

However confident I might have seemed to those around me, I was plagued by the same self-doubts as any other new doctor. Kalafong was a very busy hospital and quite soon after I started in obstetrics a baby died during birth. I could see that the professor was very upset by it. I realised that I would feel the same if something went badly wrong with one of my patients. I became so worried that I might be an inept doctor, and that a patient might die because of me, that I started to work even harder, forgetting again to eat and drink.

Lin-Lin understood how passionate I was about my work and realised that when I was working or studying, I would forget to eat. Every morning when I woke up she would have breakfast prepared, and she would even make a packed lunch for me, although I was often so absorbed that I would forget to eat it. In fact, I was so focused on my medical studies that Lin-Lin took over every other aspect of my life, even buying clothes for me because she knew I would never get round to doing it myself.

I was earning a salary of R6 540 as an intern, so I could finally buy my first car. I could not, of course, afford a new car, so I bought an old Volkswagen Fox with no air conditioning off the Combonis, but I was still very proud of it. I also rented my first studio flat and spent nearly all my spare time with Lin-Lin.

By the end of my four-month rotation in obstetrics I had managed to impress the head of the department to such an extent that he encouraged me to apply for a registrar post in obstetrics at Kalafong after I completed my compulsory year of community service. Only me and one other intern got letters of recommendation from him. It was wonderful for me, as a Medunsa student, to receive this recognition.

In South Africa crime is a constant threat, making it hard for anyone to ever completely relax. One day towards the end of my internship, Lin-Lin and I were sitting and talking in the car outside her aunt's house in Johannesburg when four guys jumped out of another car and came running towards us. I knew immediately that they were hijackers. I shouted to Lin-Lin to get out and run into the building, and the second she was out I reversed at speed. At that moment a Mercedes pulled up and the hijackers turned their attention to that vehicle.

I was in such a state that I drove all the way to Pretoria in second gear at 120 kilometres per hour. It was the closest I had come yet to being killed on the streets, and I suffered from acute stress disorder for about six months as a result. I often got panic attacks and sweaty palms when I was in my car and a group of men I didn't know approached it.

Knowing how easily my life could be ended at any moment only spurred me on to work even harder. I always want to be sure I reach my goals before it is too late. Perhaps that was why I used to run everywhere as a child and why I have never stopped rushing since.

I finished my internship at Kalafong Hospital at the same time as Lin-Lin finished her final year of medical school, and we decided that it would be a good time to get engaged. She told her family back in Myanmar and her aunts who worked as general practitioners in South Africa, but they were all horrified at the thought. They told her that she could not marry me. One of her relatives had been married to a Ugandan doctor, and they ended up getting divorced after having two daughters together, Perhaps they were afraid the same thing would happen to Lin-Lin and me.

When Lin-Lin refused to take any notice, her family contacted the Myanmar embassy, which told her that they could not give her a permit to work in South Africa after she graduated, and that she had to go back to Myanmar to get the necessary documents. She left in December 2005, but when she arrived in her home country she discovered it was a trick. Her family confiscated her passport and she was trapped.

Our love, however, was too strong to be broken that easily and we stayed in close touch, looking for ways that we could outwit her family and be together.

11 A SAD REUNION

In 2006 I moved to the farming community of Bethal in Mpu-malanga for my year of compulsory community service at the provincial hospital in the town, where I again learned much about the practice of being a doctor.

One day a young woman came in with an ectopic pregnancy and had to be operated on urgently. However, things went wrong during the anaesthetic, which was performed by one of the medical officers, and led to the death of the patient before the procedure. I was angry because she was so young. This made me interested in anaesthetics, and I underwent further training in this field during my community-service year. Still, I didn't feel like that was what I wanted to do for the rest of my life.

Although I had not yet made up my mind as to what I wanted to specialise in, I knew that I had found my calling. Being a doctor fitted perfectly with my scientific approach to life, which was in stark contrast to the superstitions I had been exposed to in child-hood. In medicine, you cannot blame your neighbour if you start coughing; you need to look at the symptoms scientifically, diagnose them correctly and then treat them.

In medicine we aim to identify and name every disease. If it

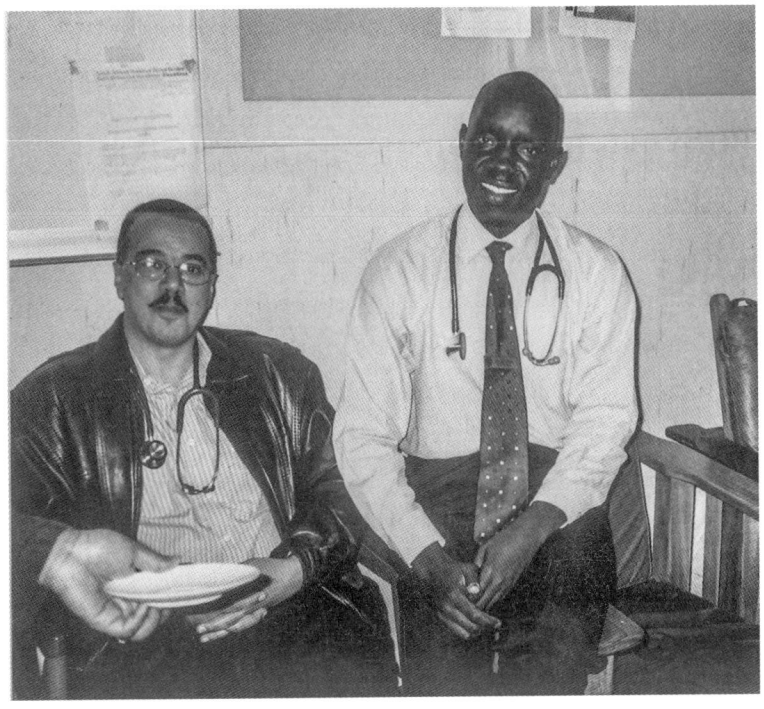

At Bethal Hospital in 2007 with another doctor

doesn't have a name, you won't know how to treat it. One of the things that I love about medicine is that it helps me to understand life. If you cannot identify an ill in society, you won't be able to find a solution and deal with it. I have often thought that the problem in South Sudan is that we're still struggling to figure out exactly what our problem is. Everyone thinks it's poverty, but we should be asking ourselves what causes that poverty when we have so many healthy young men and women with no mental problems.

In 2005 a peace agreement was signed between North and South Sudan, which paved the way for South Sudan's independence six years later. The following year, in 2006, a number of officials from the newly formed government of South Sudan came to South Africa to attend a capacity-building programme sponsored by the international community. Among them was SPLA spokesperson Samson Kwaje, whom I had first met in Asmara, and SPLA liaison Benjamin Marial Barnabas, who had assisted me in Zimbabwe after he met me in Asmara.

Benjamin invited me to join the group, and that is how I met a number of people, including Salva Kiir, then president of the government of South Sudan and deputy president of Sudan. Samson remembered me from Asmara, but we never spoke about the time I called him from Moyale and he ignored me. I decided it wouldn't serve any purpose to mention the incident.

I also met Beatrice Khamisa Wani-Noah, the wife of Dr John Tabayi, who was working for the UN in 1995 when I was in Addis Ababa. Of course John couldn't remember the scruffy boy who had tried to get his attention and help all those years ago, and I didn't blame him for it. I became good friends with Beatrice, who is currently the minister of foreign affairs for South Sudan. She and John have come to my house a few times during their visits to South Africa.

During this time, I became an informal liaison officer for the government of South Sudan, since the country didn't yet have any diplomatic representation in South Africa. I took care of most of their needs, helping the newly appointed ministers and officials to get medical treatment, driving them around and arranging accommodation for them. I was even invited to a dinner at the Union Buildings in Pretoria with then President Thabo

Mbeki. I happened to be standing beside Salva Kiir when he was interviewed on television, which led many people to believe I was a man with good connections.

Even though it was taxing, I drove up and down between Bethal and Pretoria that year because I was keen to be of service. I had seen how much a good government could achieve in South Africa during the Mbeki era and I wanted to do anything I could to help South Sudan achieve the same. I wanted to show all these visiting ministers and dignitaries what was possible, in the hope of inspiring them to improve the infrastructure of our own country.

However, I was shocked to discover evidence of nepotism, corruption and tribalism, as some of the officials brought family members from the village to join the capacity-building programme, even though many couldn't even write or speak English.

Meanwhile my brother Joseph was prospering in South Sudan. Some of the money from my sponsor, Franz Pahl, went towards helping him to build his business and some to pay for my youngest sister, Sarah, to study auditing in Khartoum. Joseph had already shown himself to be an enterprising businessman and had also helped Sarah with her school fees.

Having worked for a number of years as a bus conductor, Joseph started buying and selling petrol in cans, gradually building up the quantities he traded in and the size of the cans he used. He moved on to selling spare parts for cars and bought a container to store them in and to use as a workshop. By that time he was buying vehicles, such as buses from Kampala, and doing them up.

My brother Joseph

He had also opened a bar. It was really just a shack by the side of the road where he sold water and alcohol during the day and food in the evenings, but it provided him with another source of income. He managed to buy a couple of plots of land and taught himself to be a mechanic, so that he could service and repair the cars he bought. He wanted to be self-sufficient because he knew that if he hired other people to do the work, they would inevitably end up stealing from him.

He was a hard worker and a good businessman and I felt

confident that he would be a good person to look after any money that I was able to send back to South Sudan for the family. Among other things, he bought some land for us, part of which we wanted to use to build a house for our mother and any members of the family she might want to take under her wing. He called me a few days before Christmas to tell me how much he wanted to see me after so many years. I told him I would come home for a visit in January.

Three days later, on 23 December 2006, Sarah rang to tell me that Joseph had been taken to hospital with malaria.

'But he is doing well,' she assured me in her gentle voice.

The next day she rang again to tell me that our brother had died. I couldn't understand how that could have happened so suddenly. I wanted to be there to ask questions but I wasn't able to get a flight until after Christmas. On 27 December, I was on my first flight ever as a commercial passenger and travelling on a UN passport.

This was the first time I had been back to my homeland and, though it was a death in the family that brought me back, I had expected that it would be a joyful experience to return to my roots. Instead, I felt deeply saddened by what I saw, adding to the grief I was already experiencing for my lost brother.

My cousin and childhood friend Yaka came to fetch me at Juba airport. I was struck by the heat when I stepped off the plane, and I discovered there were no bathrooms in the terminal building. On the way to Joseph's house I noticed that there were still no tarmac roads to speak of. It was depressing to be back to crashing through potholes in clouds of dust. In my ignorance I had imagined that South Sudan would have progressed at least a little during the decade I had been away. In fact, nothing had changed at all. The country had gone backwards while the rest of the world had moved forwards.

People were still living in the same mud huts that I remembered from my childhood. Why had no one started to build with bricks or put glass in the windows? Why was there still no electricity for most people, except the generators for government premises, and no flush toilets anywhere? Even the bottled water was all imported from Uganda, and food was horribly expensive for the millions of people earning a few dollars a day. A can of Coke could cost as much as $6 (about R90). Inflation was making it impossible for ordinary people to survive.

There seemed to be nothing good going on anywhere. Everybody was praying to God for divine intervention, and the churches were full of people expecting miracles. Even the president and his ministers were praying, without realising that they needed to make decisions. Leadership was needed to develop the country, and to stop corruption and nepotism. They needed to educate a new generation and create a foundation for everyone, irrespective of their tribe, religion or language. Aid money had been pumped into South Sudan from the West, but it had been siphoned off by all the wrong people in the government. If you wanted to buy a piece of land it would cost you $100 000, ten times the price of a similar-size piece of land in relatively affluent South Africa.

I couldn't understand it. It wasn't as if the country's leaders didn't know that the rest of the world had moved on. They had all been to South Africa, the United States and European countries. They had all been treated in top-class hospitals and stayed in five-star hotels, so why could they not make it possible for their own people to progress? Some of them had even been privileged enough to be educated overseas, and had seen what fantastic strides are possible through hard work, but still they did not work hard for their own people. It seemed to me that most people in Africa who obtained a degree had at least an honorary certificate in corruption and destructive behaviour. They appeared to deliberately choose to do the wrong things. I wondered if I even belonged there any more.

Many of the men who had become leaders of the country had done so by taking up arms, recruiting soldiers and killing people. Having proved they were 'strong' men, they were given jobs in government. But, apparently, the only reason they wanted those jobs was for the money, the power and the prestige that came with them. I got the sense that in their hearts none of them wanted to do anything to help build their country and lift up their people. Although many people realised this, they believed they were unable to change things, and they were frightened to do the right thing in case the men with guns killed them and their families.

It was chaos when Yaka and I arrived at Joseph's house. The news had spread that I would be there that day and people had descended on the house, both to see me and because they were expecting a second funeral, where food would be served to everyone. I wasn't feeling well and only remember how anxious my mother was about me, and how she tried her best to keep me away from everyone. On the one hand, she was worried that people would ask me for money, and, on the other, she was still her old superstitious self and was fearful that someone might put a curse on me or poison me. It was not how I had imagined our reunion would be after so many years.

I also met my brother's pregnant wife, Margaret Yangy, and his children at the second funeral, which eventually lasted several days. There were many tears. While I was away my brother had reached out to our father's family, and many of them were there, wanting to run his funeral. I didn't have any personal issues with them, but I had never really liked any of them, perhaps because they had never been there to help us when we were children.

After the church service my father's family were drinking everything they could find in Joseph's bar, but none of them had any idea if it had been paid for or not. I could imagine the suppliers turning up at the widow's door in a few weeks demanding their money or their products back, so I locked everything away, which made them all very angry. They told me I was too young to make such decisions on behalf of the whole family and stormed off, cursing me as they went (just as my mother had feared they would).

Uncle Alex

I spent the night at Uncle Alex's house, where I had to use a bucket toilet and an outside shower again. It didn't take me long to realise I wasn't used to this kind of life any more, and I was briefly overcome with a wave of helplessness. Uncle Alex was apparently living a better life than most people in the area, but in the land of the blind a one-eyed man is king.

One of the few pleasant surprises was finding that my beloved grandmother was still alive. I was told that she had never stopped asking after me in all the years that I was away. I took her a gift of coffee, which was her favourite thing, and a blanket. When I was a child, we used to get up early to collect the coffee beans that fell off the lorries transporting them from the plantations around the village to the markets in Juba. Sometimes we could collect as much as ten kilograms in one morning, some of which I would proudly present to my grandmother. She would then roast the beans in a pan on the fire until they were black, then grind them and mix them with water. She would keep adding more water and five or six spoons of sugar until it seemed completely tasteless to me, but she loved it.

The door to her mud hut was so low I had to crouch down to get in, and she recognised my voice even before she saw me.

'Now I will die a happy woman,' she told me as she embraced me tightly. She must have been in her nineties by then, and she had lived exactly the same way every day of her life, wearing sec-ond-hand clothes, living in a dark, mud house, never using a flush toilet and eating the same food. I made it just in time – a mere four weeks later she died.

I still had told my family nothing about my journey to South Africa and the months I had spent living on the streets or locked in prison cells. Nor had I told them about the years of hard studying and the many disappointments and setbacks. No one ever asked me any detailed questions about the ten years that had gone by.

I was relieved, because I didn't want to talk about it. Not only was I ashamed about some of the things that had happened to me, such as the times I was jailed, but at this point in my life I preferred to forget about all my hardships.

As far as they knew, I had left home and had immediately been lucky enough to be taken in by the Combonis, become a doctor and make money. The problem in South Sudan is that people think that if they are not lucky enough to be given everything on a plate, then it is not their fault if they fail. They don't realise that they can achieve whatever they want if they just work hard enough. If they refuse to give up trying, then the lucky breaks will come once they make the effort. Over the years I have tried to explain this to many of the younger people in the family and I know that they often resent hearing it; they prefer to accept whatever happens to them and not put up a fight.

My brother had already been buried by the time I reached Juba. This was necessary because of the heat and the lack of refrigeration facilities. Shortly after I arrived, I went to the hospital to find out what had happened. I was shocked by the levels of chaos. It was nothing like the South African hospitals I had worked in. For one, the hospital staff could not find his file. They took me to a room where the files of all deceased patients were haphazardly stacked everywhere.

'Are these files for the whole year?' I asked.

'No,' they replied, 'just this month.'

This meant there must have been around a thousand deaths each month. The hospital my brother had been taken to was not a place for healing people but rather a place to go to say goodbye to the world. When I went to look at the emergency room, I discovered that they had only one two-litre bottle of oxygen. If anyone had experienced a bronchial spasm on the premises, they would undoubtedly have died.

I realised that my brother, like thousands of others, had died not because he was sick but because of the failings of the system. When I found his file and read the notes, I realised that he most probably didn't have malaria but had most likely died of appendicitis or a ruptured viscus, both treatable. Had he been diagnosed correctly and in time, his life could have been saved.

Throughout Joseph's second funeral service, people kept talking about his death as 'the will of God' and said that 'he is now in a better place', which annoyed me. It seemed to me that they were misrepresenting God. People like my brother were dying due to the mismanagement of their illnesses and the lack of a proper health service.

The visit to my home country spurred me on to help develop South Sudan in some way, especially when I saw how many things could easily be put right if anyone cared enough to do it. This growing conviction would eventually lead to my lobbying virtually every government minister I came across in the next few years in order to convince them that we could do so much better if we just worked harder at it. The only answer I ever really got was, 'We need to make money before we can do anything,' but any money the government did make seemed to end up in corrupt hands and was never used to create and deliver services that would help people in the long term.

One of the governors I got to know, who had previously been a general, put it even more succinctly for me. 'You may be a good doctor,' he told me, 'but if you have no medicine to give people then you will be nothing. You can't buy medicines unless you have a strong economy, so you are dependent on the politicians. If they decide not to do anything to help you, then you can do nothing.'

His words made me realise it would be pointless trying to be a doctor in South Sudan until the political system, and the educational system, had been mended.

While I was at the hospital that day, searching for my brother's file, I heard that Salva Kiir, the South Sudanese president, whom I had been introduced to a few months earlier, was coming on a visit. At our first meeting he had seemed very cold, quite different from the warmth and charisma of SPLA founder John Garang. This time he came to avert a threatened strike by hospital staff, which he did by simply promising to hand over taxpayers' money as an incentive not to strike. This seemed to me a very short-term fix for a very big underlying problem.

People told me that Kiir had a good heart, but this seemed to me like a typically bad leadership decision. Leaders with poor insight into a country's problems do not make good economic decisions, however good their hearts may be. South Sudan needs leaders with insight who can make proper decisions. The poverty in South Sudan is due to poor leadership decisions and lack of direction from generation to generation. To me, dispensing government funds on a personal whim seemed like little more than a bribe and political posturing. He told the staff he didn't want them to strike because he didn't want people 'complaining', but how can you hope to improve a service if you don't listen to people's complaints?

Nearly a decade later, during my training as a fellow in the pulmonology department at Wits University, I passed him a few times in the hospital when he came to the country for treatment. I did not bother to acknowledge him, even though the ambassador, who had recently been appointed and was accompanying him, was a friend of mine. I cannot understand a leader who does nothing to improve the health care of his people, but whose conscience allows him to go to a hospital in another country for his own treatment.

After some time in Myanmar, Lin-Lin had taken a job in Australia and had moved there shortly before I went to visit my family in South Sudan. She asked me to join her, and even managed to line up a job interview for me.

After listening to the whole story, my mother asked me if I thought it was wise to make such a major life-changing decision based on my love for a woman, particularly as Lin-Lin had already shown that she did not have the strength to stand up to her family. My mother's words gave me much food for thought.

In the meantime, I had accepted a permanent position at Bethal Hospital. I also wrote my American licence exams, since I had been struggling for two years to get a South African identity document even though I already had permanent residence. Although I was committed to the African continent and felt I could still do things here, I needed to live in a country that would at least acknowledge my citizenship.

Joseph's death proved to be a turning point in my medical

career. It occurred to me that many people can become surgeons and do the cutting, but not everyone is able to make diagnoses – in the absence of things like CT scans – and be good physicians. Even as a student, I knew I was good at internal medicine and had a talent for making diagnoses. My experience at Kalafong Hospital had put me off internal medicine for a while, but after visiting South Sudan I realised that this was where my passion lay.

From the middle of 2007 I started applying to different universities to specialise in internal medicine. However, as a registrar position was a government-funded post, I needed a South African identity document to be eligible. Since I still didn't have one, my applications were rejected by Wits University and the University of Pretoria.

In August several things happened at the same time. I was offered a job at an Australian hospital but two or three weeks later I also got my South African identity document. That changed everything. I was even offered a position as director of health in the government of South Sudan, but I didn't feel qualified for it, so I didn't consider it seriously.

I urgently needed to decide what I wanted to do with my life.

I decided to stay in South Africa, and asked Lin-Lin to return now that she had got her passport back. She, however, decided that she couldn't defy her family in that way. I knew then that our relationship had run its course.

In October I took a South Sudanese minister to an old Medunsa professor of mine for treatment. My former professor asked me why I wasn't specialising, as he had been impressed by me when I was still a student and always thought I'd make a good physician.

In fact, he told me that he had insisted that I should get a distinction in internal medicine but had been overruled. I told him about my troubles.

Since I had by then received my South African identity document, he offered to write a letter of recommendation to the University of Pretoria. I collected the letter the following day. On 1 November I was accepted by the University of Pretoria to be a registrar in internal medicine for four years in the Steve Biko Academic Hospital, the teaching hospital attached to the university.

12 TRYING TO MAKE A DIFFERENCE IN SOUTH SUDAN

My four years at Steve Biko Academic Hospital taught me many valuable lessons. It was not always an easy ride, but I learned how to deal with conflict in the workplace and also with professional competitiveness and prejudice.

The environment created by the seniors at the hospital was very hostile to black registrars. Of the 18 to 24 registrars in internal medicine, only three were black. Many of the seniors came from the same culture and they felt more comfortable with people who were similar to them. It was not just the black registrars who struggled; even a Portuguese registrar suffered because he came from a different cultural background.

I had to deal with a few conflict situations. In one instance a senior wanted his own way despite the hospital rules. When I enforced the rules, as I was told to do by my superior, I was accused of not respecting authority. I was called in by the head of the department, who didn't show any understanding for my explanation and insisted that I apologise to the senior. I refused, whereupon I was instructed to go and see a psychiatrist – simply because I was outspoken and had stood up for myself. Thankfully, the psychiatrist cleared me and said I was fine.

The experience also taught me to stand on my own two feet. In order to fulfil the criteria for specialising in internal medicine, I had to complete a research project. Usually, a senior acts as a mentor for the research project, but mine was not interested in assisting me at all. So I completed it on my own a year before I finished my training.

As a registrar, you do 24-hour calls. After your call ends, you are supposed to hand over your critical patients to the next registrar on call, so that they can look after them while you get some rest before your next call. I got the sense that at our morning meetings the senior registrars would simply look for problems and opportunities to criticise me for poor management. Yet I always knew my work, and I could answer questions confidently when we did our rounds. A few of the black South African registrars ended up resigning, but I decided I would not allow myself to be intimidated. I promised myself that if they wanted to kick me out rather than give me my master's degree, I would gladly leave.

If I had had a victim mentality, my time at Steve Biko would have crushed me, but I was determined that I would not quit because of the system. Looking back, I realise I was no angel at that time of my life. I was impatient and hot-headed, but I always did my work.

It was also during my time at Steve Biko that I developed my three principles for success: passion, determination and consistency. I realised that when you are passionate about something, time loses its importance; you are driven more by getting the perfect results than by watching the clock. You find joy in whatever you are doing and are not easily discouraged by obstacles.

Life is never smooth sailing, but if you're running all day, you won't get far. Especially when you get stuck, you need determination to move forward, even if you're moving at high speed. Determination will help you to see challenges as opportunities to grow.

If you are a doctor, consistency is very important. Your patients should know that they will all get the same standard of treatment, regardless of who they are, and that you will always give them your best. As a doctor, you want consistent results.

These three things all go together. If you are passionate but not determined, you will not succeed. And even though you might be determined, if you are not consistent you will also not succeed.

I was shocked by how little had been done to help the people of South Sudan in the ten years I had been away. I vowed that, once I was successful I would return and do all I could to help develop the country, even if in only a small way. It was something I had been thinking about as an abstract concept for years, but now I could see I needed to start laying concrete plans.

I could see, however, that if I went back there to work as a doctor, I too would have nothing, just as the governor had explained to me. That would be of little help to anyone. I would have to make money somewhere else in order to be able to return and make any difference at all. Even my mother told me that it would be a mistake for me to come back to South Sudan to work as a doctor. By that time, because of the small amounts of money I was able to send her, she was at least able to stop selling alcohol.

I decided that the first thing I should do was to create a company in South Sudan to bottle clean water, so that people wouldn't have to import expensive bottled water from Uganda. I had been planning to build my mother a house, but I decided it would be better first to build a bottling plant. With the income from this, I could do other things, such as building her house. The bottling plant would create a number of good jobs and provide clean drinking water for people at lower prices.

As well as believing that it would be something good for the local community, I thought that setting up the company would provide an income to support the many members of my family who needed to study and train in order to escape poverty and become productive, useful citizens. It would also allow me to give up working in South Africa and come back to South Sudan to provide hands-on help to improve the country's infrastructure by building and running projects such as schools and hospitals. My mother would then not only have a decent brick-built house but there would also be the necessary cash flow to maintain and run it.

It seemed to me that as long as there was fighting in South Sudan, life there would never improve, but I knew that the fighting would continue until leaders emerged who had no interest in growing rich or powerful but simply wanted to help the country move forward. One of the reasons, however, that the war went on is because so many people are hungry and too poor to be able to get food to satisfy that hunger. It is hard to concentrate on making constructive long-term plans when your belly is always empty like a hyena's. It is a vicious cycle that has to be broken.

In my mind I worked out that the reasons most men fight are to get food, money and women. So if I could be part of the efforts to improve agriculture to combat hunger and poverty, I would be able to work on the long-term issues, such as improving the country's health and educational infrastructure, providing safe hospitals, clean water and flushing toilets, and sports facilities. People, particularly children, need to feel valued and loved in order to flourish, but first they have to be fed and to feel secure, and then they need to be given education.

If, for instance, I could rebuild the schools in Loka Round, where I had started my education, it would attract people back from places like Uganda and start the process of creating a well-educated new generation of citizens for the future. Once one school was up and running, I reasoned, it would be easier to raise the funds to build more. If I could achieve that, I would be putting my own education to the best possible use.

It would be important, however, that the whole community was involved in such a project, so that they would feel they had a stake in it and would feel proud of it.

In 2001 I had met a German guy called Thomas Greiten who had come to South Africa to do community service with the Comboni Missionaries. He was 20 years old at the time. We became good friends and stayed in touch when he went back to Germany to study mechanical engineering. When I returned from South Sudan in early 2007, I got in touch with Thomas and shared my plan for starting a bottled water factory with around R400 000 that I had managed to save. He liked the idea, and we drew up a business plan together.

Yaka had studied in Khartoum to become an industrial engineer during the time I had been making my way in South Africa.

While I was in South Sudan, we went back to our childhood village together to see how much was left of our first home, but the graves of his father and our grandfather were all that remained. The mud huts had melted away and the site had vanished beneath nearly 20 years of undergrowth. It was like the compound, and the years we had played there together, had never existed. Everything of value had been stripped away by looters, including the roof of the school.

We went down to the river together to talk about life and about how we could make a difference to our country. We talked non-stop; it was like we had never been apart. Our conversation left me feeling that there might be hope for the future of South Sudan if there were more people like Yaka. I asked him to join me in my plans for building a water bottling plant and he agreed. I knew we had to keep a low profile, though: whenever it becomes known that someone intends to do something to help the people of South Sudan to get ahead, others quickly move in to try to steal from them.

Yaka had not married, and we soon became very close again. Once Joseph's funeral was over, and before I set off for home, I registered the name of the bottling company, Sanaqua, as part of a holding company called Brightstar, and went back to South Africa to work on the documentation for the project.

My role in the project was to raise the necessary finance and to get to know the relevant ministers through the contacts I had made already. I spoke to quite a few, including the SPLA's Samson Kwaje and Dr John Tabayi, who both decided to invest in the project. I also met with some local doctors, who were very generous. Over time, I managed to raise about R1.5 million.

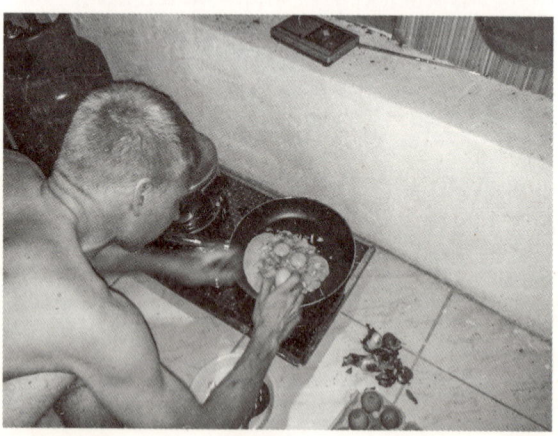

My German friend, Thomas Greiten, who helped me set up the water bottling plant in Juba. He stoically faced the basic living conditions.

We calculated that it was going to cost around R3.7 million to set the project up. Thomas agreed to come and oversee the construction phase. I returned to South Sudan in 2007 to look for land in Juba. I approached Archbishop Lukudu, who had helped me re-establish contact with my mother. He offered to lease us land from the Diocese of Juba next to a church in the Rajab East neighbourhood, where we could drill for water.

When Thomas arrived in South Sudan, around June 2007, he did not fully comprehend the lack of resources – no running water, no plumbing and no electricity – but he rose to the challenge magnificently. He brought his own food, cooking utensils and everything he needed to be independent, but he was not quite prepared for how primitive everything was, not for the intensity of the heat nor the mosquito bites nor the horror of rats gnawing at his heels as he slept. He endured all the hardships that I had known as a child, but he refused to give up.

However, as soon as the community saw a white guy arriving, they wanted money for everything. Thomas explained to everyone who would listen that it was my project, not his, but they didn't believe him. Halfway through the drilling process a group of locals, stirred up by the priest from Rajab East, came and destroyed the borehole we had drilled at a cost of $30 000 (R420 000 at the time). They believed that they were entitled to the rent for the land. This 'entitlement mentality', rather than working hard and earning the bread you eat, is a major issue in Africa and one of the reasons why poverty is so persistent. We had to admit temporary defeat and Thomas went back to Germany in December 2007.

I went back to South Sudan to talk to Archbishop Lukudu about the troublesome priest. It took him a year to have the priest removed. During this time the project stood still. Archbishop Lukudu managed to find another piece of land close to the first plot and acted as our contact and facilitator with the local community.

The rental was supposed to be $4 500 a month (around R33 000) for two hectares of land with absolutely nothing on it. There was no option to negotiate; it was a matter of 'take it or leave it'. This is another reason why it is so difficult to start a business in a country like South Sudan, and why most investors find it unattractive.

All this time, while I was trying to set up the water bottling plant in Juba, I was still working as a registrar at Steve Biko Academic Hospital. It wasn't easy to juggle all my commitments. At least while the project was on hold, I could focus on my work at the hospital.

In November 2008, Barack Obama was elected president of the United States. I watched every second of the coverage of the election results, which meant staying up all night with my sister Sarah, who was visiting at the time. I knew it was foolish to lose a night's sleep but I just couldn't take my eyes off the television screen.

When Obama won it felt like a personal victory to me, like my own father had just become president. Not only was he young and black and had relatives in East Africa, but he also held out hope to me: someone whom no one would have believed had the potential to become the leader of the free world had succeeded in doing so. He had come from nowhere, just like me, which showed that worldly success no longer had to be about colour or where you were born. It was all about where you were going and how hard you worked to get there. He gave himself no limits and reinforced my belief that anything was possible.

Obama also showed enormous emotional intelligence and never resorted to aggression to win his arguments. He handled all criticism with great dignity and intelligence. He was a beacon of hope and inspired me to work even harder in the hope of achieving something really great with my life.

The day after Obama's election victory I was on call for cardiology, but having sat up all night with Sarah I fell asleep at ten o'clock the next evening and didn't hear my phone ringing until four in the morning. When they were unable to reach me, the hospital had to call out one of my colleagues. The following morning I faced a disciplinary hearing. Aware that it was my fault that I had missed a whole night's sleep, I took responsibility and resigned on the spot.

One of the professors called me to her office when she heard about the incident, and talked me down. I never made that mistake again.

In 2009 Pope Benedict XVI named Father Sandri as Bishop of Witbank, which meant that the man who had been my role model since the day I met him, and who was the closest thing I had to a father figure, was back in the country. On every serious matter in my life, it was always Father Sandri who I turned to for wise advice.

Setting up a business in a country with no established business culture is always hard. Every aspect of the water bottling venture was an uphill struggle. Thomas and I had worked out that it would be cheaper to buy a prefabricated factory structure and transport it to Sudan than trying to build one there. So in early 2009 we bought the structure, which was worth about R1 million. I had already bought a truck for the company, though I was unaware that it had been involved in an accident and was not strong enough to carry the structure.

In the second half of 2009 I hired a company to organise a driver to take the truck from South Africa through Botswana, Zambia and on to South Sudan. The owner of the company, whom I had met through his wife, who was a professional nurse at Steve Biko, turned out to be dishonest. Two weeks into the trip, he told me the truck had already reached Tanzania. He wanted me to pay him the balance of the fee.

He never paid the driver. However, the driver used his cellphone to call me. He was still in Botswana, having run out of fuel, and had not been given money to buy more. I was furious when I discovered I was being cheated, but I still managed to get money directly to the driver to buy fuel. He set off again but then ran into mechanical trouble in southern Zambia. Since I was on rotation at Steve Biko, a friend named Ed Marchand kindly offered to fly up to Zambia with spare parts. However, when the driver got to Lusaka in October, the truck broke down. We were stuck *again*.

Just when I was starting to become completely despondent, my luck changed. A Yugoslavian guy called Bob happened to be driving past in his truck when he saw mine stranded by the side of the road. Pulling over, he asked the driver where the owner was, and was told that I was in South Africa. He took my number and called to tell me that he thought it was likely my truck and the prefab structure would soon be stolen if something wasn't done. He suggested that he take the tractor unit to his yard in Lusaka and then tow the trailer with the prefab structure to a nearby police station for safekeeping.

'How much is this going to cost?' I asked suspiciously. 'Because I have no money left.'

'No charge,' he said in a thick Balkan accent, 'I'm just helping out.'

I was so amazed and impressed by his kind gesture that I was happy to trust him, and he did exactly what he promised. I had to raise some more money to repair the truck, which I did from the African Bank. In December I bought parts for the engine, which cost R70 000, packed them up carefully and flew them to Zambia. I went there myself, sleeping in the truck while I got things sorted out, and Yugoslavian Bob found an engineer who could do the repairs.

My next problem was raising money for diesel to get to Juba. But Bob, in another extraordinarily trusting gesture, said he would lend me the money both for the fuel and to pay the driver to complete the trip.

'You can pay me back when you get back to South Africa,' he said.

'I will pay you in three months,' I promised.

I never found out what motivated him to be so helpful and so trusting. He didn't know me, and I could easily have changed my number and disappeared without repaying his money. I will be forever grateful that he turned up where and when he did and decided to come to my rescue. It did a great deal to restore my confidence in human nature at a time when so many people were undermining it. It reminded me of the day I found the money lying in the road when I was a child. I had assumed it was a gift from God. I was grateful

191

to Bob not only for the loan but also for restoring my hopes for the future. If everyone behaved in such a generous way the world would be a wonderful place indeed.

In January 2010 the truck was repaired and the driver set off again. He was held up at several points on his journey to the border between Kenya and South Sudan. The driver kept telling me that he needed money to bribe the police and get across the various borders. Eventually, I became suspicious and established that all the money I had been sending him for fuel was sitting untouched in his bank account. He had not been paying anyone anything.

By the time the three months were up and I needed to repay Bob, I had run out of money. I had a second-hand BMW, which was my pride and joy, so I sold it and paid Bob what I owed him. Then I bought a new car, paying for it in instalments, which was the worst idea ever. I had grown used to having no money. For the first 28 or so years of my life, my main concerns were getting enough to eat and paying school and university fees. I was now discovering that it was even more stressful to have no money after taking on responsibilities and commitments to other people. I was becoming desperate. I even tried buying lottery tickets to make a bit more money to keep the business moving forward, but, as any sensible person would guess, that didn't work.

On top of that, the shareholders in Sanaqua were now asking for their money back, since the project didn't seem to be happening. People who had been my friends started to turn against me because they felt I owed them money, just like what had happened when I tried to be an entrepreneur as a child. I was terrified that I might again end up in prison. I called my mother about my problems, knowing that she hadn't yet spent all the money I had sent her from my sponsor, Franz Pahl.

'Come home,' she told me. 'We can slaughter a cow to make up for the sins of your father and lift the curse.'

'Rather than ritually slaughter a poor cow, Mom,' I said, 'it might be better for you to lend me the money that the cow would cost.'

She told me she still had about $2 000 of the money I had sent her. When I next went up to Juba, in February 2010, she sent me out to the foul-smelling latrine behind the house. She had hidden the money in the roof. I had to admit it was a clever hiding place, since no thief was likely to want to spend time searching in a stink like that. I was grateful to her for coming to my rescue, just as she had done when I was a child and needed bailing out, but I felt disappointed in myself. I wanted to be the one helping her after all her years of self-sacrifice, not the other way round.

Now that I had some money, I decided that I would go to meet the truck and confront the driver in Nadapal, a town on the border between South Sudan and Kenya. The truck was stuck there because the customs officials were asking for yet another bribe, which I said I wouldn't pay.

One of my friends, Ed Marchand, gave me his old Nissan and, at my mother's suggestion, I asked Yaka to go with me to the Kenyan border. Because Yaka had been in the army, I think she believed he would protect me. I later found out that he had slid a pistol under his seat without my seeing as we headed south. Just in case ...

As we drove, I noticed that the whites of Yaka's eyes were yellow. I remembered that we had both contracted hepatitis when we were seven or eight years old. Mine had cleared up, but his obviously hadn't, and now he was looking chronically jaundiced. He was going to need treatment. I thought I would have to persuade him to come to South Africa once our operation was over.

I was probably driving too fast on potholed roads for such an old car. One of the bolts that attached the engine to the chassis worked loose, causing the engine to suddenly slip down, making the car list to one side, which caused a tyre to burst. We screeched to a wobbly halt. It took me a while to put on the spare wheel, and we set off again at a more sedate pace, but a few kilometres further on the new tyre picked up a puncture. I couldn't continue on a flat tyre, and so I had to take the wheel off again and set off to roll both of them for ten kilometres along the side of the road to the nearest garage. By that stage Yaka was not looking at all well. I could see he would not be able to take on such a physical challenge, so I told him to wait with the car.

Trying to keep both wheels rolling simultaneously in the same direction without losing control was a major challenge, and I spent most of the time chasing one or other into the bush as it careered off the road. About halfway to the garage a truck driver very kindly stopped to give me a lift the rest of the way.

At the garage I got both tyres fixed and managed to find a lift back. I was too tired to physically roll the wheels any further. I replaced the one wheel, put the spare in the boot and we set out once more, but a few miles down the road the same thing happened again. By then I was too exhausted to do any more wheel-changing, so we limped on until we found a village where there were some people sitting under a tree. They watched us approach with lazy, curious eyes and we asked them if we could leave the car with them while we hitched a lift to the border with another driver.

On the way to the border, Yaka tried to convince me to pay the bribe to release the truck. Having been in the army, he understood better than me the way such things might play out.

'You have to pay it,' he told me, 'or they might well kill us.'

I was pretty sure he was exaggerating so I continued to refuse. I have never liked being part of a culture where paying bribes is considered a normal way to do business. It just feels completely wrong to me when all my documents were in order and I had done all the right, law-abiding things.

'Everyone pays bribes,' the soldiers told me when I protested. 'Who do you think you are not to pay?'

'But we are all South Sudanese now,' I said, trying to reason with them. 'We should all be working together.'

They were not going to give in and Yaka pointed out that if I didn't pay they might damage the truck, so I reluctantly gave in and paid the $300 they were asking for. Climbing into the cab with the driver, we drove to the village where we had left the car, fixed the tyre and then set out very slowly for Juba behind the truck. As we came into a village about half an hour from the border, the truck driver accidentally went the wrong way round a tyre placed in the road to denote a roundabout.

We were waved to a stop by a policeman who was sitting by the side of the road sipping tea with his colleagues. He fined the truck driver another $500. I was pretty sure they had put the tyre there simply in order to stop people and extort money. When I told the policeman I didn't have that much money he took away the car keys, eventually agreeing to return them for $250. I could see that it was pointless trying to stick to my principles under such conditions.

We took the car to a workshop to get the engine fixed and went to look for somewhere cheap to sleep. It was midnight. Yaka found a guesthouse owned by some people he knew, which was actually just a mud hut next to a church. It was very dirty and was going to use up all the money we had left, so I said I would rather sleep in the car.

'You're from South Africa,' he protested. 'You need to sleep in a nice bed. I have found this place and you are being ungrateful.'

We were both so angry after everything we had been through during the day that neither of us would give in. I slept in the car while he stayed in the guesthouse. In the morning he wanted some-thing to eat but I told him it was too early and we had to get back to Juba. More policemen demanded bribes before they would allow the truck into the city.

That night I decided I would have to accept defeat, put the Sanaqua project on hold again and try to refund the shareholders. The project was taking up too much of my time and money, and I needed to concentrate on my medicine and my studies. I felt very sad at having already spent a lot of the start-up money on salaries, with nothing to show for it.

13 A WEDDING AND A FUNERAL

One day in mid 2009, while I was juggling my work at Steve Biko Academic Hospital and trying to set up the water bottling plant in Juba, I got to the medical library just outside the hospital a few minutes too late. I urgently needed to take out a particular book, but the librarian on the desk was in a foul mood and told me I would have to come back the next day. I promised I would read the book overnight and bring it back in the morning, but still she refused, stubbornly sticking to the letter of the library rules. However, she did say I could try to ask her colleague.

I got a call on my pager to go back to the ICU. The librarian's colleague, a very attractive girl who introduced herself as Motheo, saw how distressed I was. After pleading with her, Motheo kindly signed out the book for me. I was deeply grateful for this gesture and we chatted for a few moments before I had to dash away. When I took the book back the next day, she made a great impression on me with her soft-spoken kindness.

It was only when I ran into her in the ward later that day that I discovered she was also working in the hospital, as a physiotherapy student. Her smile when she saw me made me brave and I asked her out. We started dating and I soon fell in love with the beautiful and

Above: My two Ugandan friends, Dr Charles Echelu (left) and Dr Joseph Adrigwe, who negotiated the dowry for Motheo on my behalf.

Left: Motheo and I on our first date in 2009

vivacious Motheo. As I got to know her better, I learned that both her parents were teachers, but her father had been killed in a road accident when she was just eight years old.

Motheo fell pregnant after we had been dating for a few months. I still remember clearly the fear I felt in the pit of my stomach when I went to the clinic with her and saw the ultrasound images of the tiny life growing inside her. At that stage I wasn't even sure if I should ever marry. I was so dedicated to my work and couldn't see how I would find time for family life. I was also unsure whether I would ever feel comfortable telling my life story to my kids.

My worst nightmare would be not being able to earn enough

to provide for them and to find that I was no better than my own father. I was broke again after my failed business venture, and I was terrified that any child I had would suffer the same start in life that I'd had. The first thing I did when I got home from the scan was to buy life insurance, to make sure that the baby would still be able to get an education whatever might happen to me.

When I told Motheo's mother and her family early in 2010 that I wanted to marry her, they asked to meet my family. I had no one in South Africa, so instead I asked Dr Charles Echelu and Dr Joseph Adrigwe from Uganda to go and negotiate an appropriate dowry. The family agreed to accept a very reasonable sum, except that I still didn't have any money because of the debts incurred over the truck. So I had to go back to the African Bank and take out yet another loan at an extortionate rate of interest.

We had a traditional wedding ceremony in March that year, and at the end of July our daughter Naledi was born. We decided that once we'd settled into our new roles as parents we'd also have a Western wedding. The date was set for 15 October 2011. At that point I was heavily indebted but I didn't want to burden Motheo with this information, as she was just starting out as a physiotherapist and had high hopes of improving our lifestyle and giving Naledi the best in life.

I had just over a year to save enough money for the wedding celebrations and to pay for my mother and uncle to come from South Sudan for the ceremony. Both Motheo and I took on whatever extra work we could find to try to get together some money with which to establish our family unit. We were exploited by a number of people we worked for because we were desperate, and everyone could see that.

A friend of mine had just opened a private practice in Witbank (today Emalahleni) and was very busy, seeing 40 or 50 patients a day, so I asked him if he could give me some work over the weekends. I earned him about R50 000 each weekend, and treated the patients very well, but he only gave me about R2 500, even though I had to pay a lot for petrol to travel to and from Witbank, which was an hour's drive away. Motheo was earning more money than me as a physiotherapist.

Somehow we managed to scrape together enough money to pay for everything and even to go on honeymoon. That taught me the power of planning: even when you have nothing, you can still plan for something special.

To my delight, Bishop Sandri agreed to marry us. During the ceremony, he told the story of how he and I had first met at the Cathedral of Christ the King, in Johannesburg. He described my complete lack of possessions and my refusal to give up on my dream of getting an education. The story obviously came as a shock to all those present, none of whom, including Motheo, knew the full extent of my early struggles.

I was deeply embarrassed to have the poverty of my beginnings exposed like that, but of course the Bishop knew that I should be proud, not ashamed, of where I had come from and how far I had travelled. It would be several years before I read *The Alchemist* by Paulo Coelho and realised that my journey out of poverty and through adversity was nothing to be embarrassed about. Only then did I see that there had always been a purpose in everything that befell me. The setbacks I had encountered had fuelled my determination to do something to improve my chances in life, each one reinforcing the steel of resolve in my soul.

Today I know that I have gotten as far as I have only because of the adversity I have faced. If I had been born into a comfortable life in Khartoum, Nairobi or Kampala, I don't believe I would have gone so far or grown so much. I think people only stretch themselves to their limits when they are forced to. As a result, most people only fulfil a small part of their potential.

It was a wonderful wedding day, and afterwards Motheo and I travelled to Venice for a romantic honeymoon. It was our first trip to Europe and a magical time.

With the added responsibility of a wife and a baby, I needed to take my work even more seriously. I went to Steve Biko Hospital and told them that I wanted a full-time job there or else I would go into private practice, but they told me they had nothing for me. Then, in August 2011, Professor James Ker called to tell me that the Highveld Mediclinic in Trichardt, a small town close to Secunda in Mpumalanga, was possibly looking for a private practitioner.

'Are you going to recommend me?' I asked.

'Yes,' he replied.

Professor Ker, a pulmonologist, advised me to spend a few years establishing myself, both professionally and financially, so that I could then specialise in whatever I decided was my area of interest.

One long weekend in September, I was asked to help out at Highveld Mediclinic. I successfully treated many patients, and nurses and patients alike were very positive in their responses. Based on

A family photo taken on our wedding day (left to right): Kola Tlotleng, Lapheus Phalatse, Lucas Phalatse, Helen Adrigwe, Kealeboga Sedidi, a family friend, Utlwile Sedidi, Obakeng Sedidi, Joseph Adrigwe, Phoebe Kiden (my mother), Enike Losuk, Elizabeth Phalatse, Mathudi Nkoliswa.

this feedback, the hospital manager, Willem Schoonbee, realised that I was really dedicated and passionate and he offered me a doctor's room. He said he would provide everything I needed to set up a practice in the hospital, at a time when I could not possibly have afforded to do so myself. He even helped me to rent a house next to the hospital, which would become our family home for the next five years. Willem said I could start on 1 November 2011.

Motheo and I had just returned from our honeymoon when we spent our first night in the house in Trichardt. We had to sleep on the floor because the van moving our furniture was delayed and we couldn't afford a hotel. The house, which was just outside the hospital gates, also gave Motheo the space to set up her physiotherapy practice.

With Naledi on our wedding day

Willem's offer was the greatest demonstration of faith that anyone had ever shown in me. Later, when he fell ill, he even asked me to care for him. I will never be able to thank him enough for his courage in giving me that opportunity. In my first month in the practice, I earned as much as I had previously made in a whole year.

There was no other black doctor working as an internist at Highveld Mediclinic at the time. I think the other doctors there at first felt sure that none of their white and Indian patients would want to be seen by me, a black doctor. Once my reputation started to grow, however, patients who had never previously considered going to a black doctor began asking for me, and in 2012 this caused some friction with one colleague in particular. He had been there for many years, and whenever I saw a patient, he would claim it was his patient, forgetting that the patient could choose which doctor they wanted to see. I suspect he felt threatened that I would take business away from him. He would try to change my prescriptions and tell the patients that I was his junior, but in private practice there is no ranking. It got so bad that at one point I wanted to leave, but after giving it some proper thought I decided I would not be driven out or bullied. Willem was incredibly skilful at dealing with the conflicts tactfully and fairly. I also made sure that I provided a better service than anyone else, so that all my patients would speak up for me.

I also received excellent advice from Bishop Sandri on the matter. He used to like me to sit with him and watch sport, and he particularly enjoyed horse racing. One day when I visited him in Witbank and we were watching races, I told him about my situation.

'Can you see the horses?' he said. 'What do you see?'

'They are all running,' I said, unable to understand what he was asking.

'Look again,' he said. 'Look at the one in the lead. Is he looking around at the others coming up behind?'

'No.'

'Exactly, he is just running his own race. Doing the best he can. He doesn't care whether he wins or not, but still he is going to win. That's what you need to do. Just run your own race and don't worry about what the others are doing.'

His message was that I should focus on my work, on what was at hand, and not on the person causing the conflict. Looking back now, I can see that such conflicts with colleagues, which caused me enormous emotional stress at the time, made me a better doctor. They made me question everything I did, to be sure I did it right, and made me determined to be more conscientious than anyone else, so that they would never be able to criticise the care I provided.

Eventually, I was given my own medical ward with a team of nurses, who were as passionate as me about providing a high level of care. In a very short time we had 100 per cent occupancy. Everyone who worked there was willing to put in as many hours as necessary to provide the highest level of care.

Articles began to appear in the local media in which patients talked about the high standard of service I provided, and my workload grew ferociously as a result. I was still determined to give every patient as much time and attention as they needed, regardless of how many hours that might mean I had to work. When the authorities came to do an audit of all the doctors in the hospital, they couldn't understand how it was possible that one doctor could see so many patients. Willem explained to them that it was simply because I put in more hours than anyone else.

The fact that I was black was a problem at the start. Many white people in South Africa are still reluctant to go to black doctors, whereas black and Indian people don't mind what colour their doctors are. I had to work twice as hard to prove myself, but it paid off and I soon had an incredibly busy schedule. I was working 16 hours a day or more, seven days a week, and never taking a holiday. I was very happy to do that.

One day, a white patient broached a sensititve matter.

'Of course,' I said, a little nervously.

'You are the only black man I would ever trust. You are too good to be black.'

I know that he intended to pay me a compliment, but he seemed entirely unaware that in doing so he was insulting all my friends, relatives and fellow citizens across Africa. In a way, though, I am grateful to him for his honesty. He was inadvertently expressing feelings that I am well aware are still shared by a large number of white people in South Africa and beyond. Perhaps if everyone was as open and honest about their prejudices as that patient was, we could start to work on helping people to see life more clearly.

I would never have been able to establish my practice at Highveld Mediclinic so quickly and so successfully without Motheo's support. I was able to work such long hours because she took over the running of our household, from changing light bulbs to overseeing the gardening and doing most of the parenting, while also having a full-time job. We always tried to save money by doing things ourselves, and one night she surprised a group of friends by knowing the price of a bag of cement (we were busy renovating our patio at the time).

In 2012 I was invited by a drug company to a medical congress in Beijing. The work ethic of the Chinese people impressed me immediately when I saw the transformation of their great cities, but it seemed best illustrated by the age and scale of the Great Wall. That something so enormous and long-lasting could be built by hand filled me with awe, and made me wonder yet again why we have been so incapable of building anything of lasting substance in South Sudan. Not only had someone had the idea in the first place, but they had also acted on it. They had completed the task, no matter the cost. We have many great ideas in South Sudan, but nobody dares to turn them into action.

Before leaving for China I brought Yaka to South Africa. I had been told that he was seriously ill. He had become secretary-general of Equatorian Youth and played a big role in the process of composing a national anthem for South Sudan. He had finally married a few months before. When he arrived at the airport, he could barely walk. I had not realised that his condition had deteriorated so much. We headed straight for Highveld Mediclinic where I had an MRI scan and other tests done.

As we drove from the airport, he asked, 'Do our leaders not come to this country? Do they not see these roads?'

'They do,' I replied, 'and they all blame the government for not doing more, forgetting that when they become ministers, they are the government. According to them it is always the fault of someone else. No one actually takes responsibility for making anything happen – not in the general population and not among the leaders either. Everyone consumes whatever they are given but no one works hard to make more of whatever it is that is needed for the future.'

The cover of the funeral programme for my
childhood friend Thomas (Yaka)

Once we started doing tests, we discovered that Yaka had stage four carcinomas affecting his liver and lungs. His condition was terminal … my childhood friend was dying. We decided it would be best for him to return home to South Sudan to be with his family. I bought him a business-class ticket so he would be comfortable during the flight, and I travelled with him.

When we arrived in South Sudan, however, his family were very angry at me because I hadn't cured him. In their ignorance, they made me the enemy. I left after a day as I had to go on to the conference in China. Yaka died about two weeks later, leaving behind his wife, who was pregnant with their daughter. It was a great loss to me.

Early in 2013 I set about designing and building a house for my mother, importing all the materials from South Africa. In March of that year I decided to visit Juba to see how the house was progressing. They were just finishing off the tiles and the plastering. My mother was happier than I had ever seen her, but she eventually confessed that she was still suffering from a burning sensation in her stomach, like heartburn.

When she had visited South Africa for our wedding two years earlier, I had taken her to a cardiologist for a checkup because she had been complaining about gastric pains. However, the specialist gave her the all clear and she returned to South Sudan.

Mom was supposed to visit us in South Africa a few weeks later, when Motheo was due to give birth to our second child. I decided to take her for another medical checkup once she arrived in the country. What she didn't tell me was that she had fallen and lost consciousness a week earlier. If she had told me that, I would have guessed that she was developing problems with diabetes and high blood pressure.

On 19 April 2013 she called me while I was at work, which was a very unusual thing for her to do.

'I just wanted to say thank you so much for the house,' she said.

'It's not finished yet,' I laughed. 'Wait until it is complete and then you can move in and you will have the perfect life.'

'I just wanted to say thank you for that.'

On 21 April, Sarah called to tell me that Mom had collapsed and been taken to the hospital. I can only assume that Mom didn't want to tell me she was ill because she didn't want to cause me distress. I wish she had told me. If I had known, I could have done something about it.

'Why is she in hospital?' I asked, remembering what they said about Joseph when he went in.

'She has malaria.'

That made me panic. 'She has been living in South Sudan all her life,' I said. 'She has been getting malaria all this time. Why is this different? There's something else wrong.'

'No, she's fine,' Sarah insisted. 'She's just lying here beside me.'

'Can I speak to her?'

'She says no because she can't hear well because they are giving her a high dose of quinine.'

'Can I talk to the doctor?'

'He won't be back till tomorrow morning.'

'Do I need to book a flight and get her to Nairobi?'

'No, she's fine.'

The next day, the hospital discharged her, but she collapsed in the car on the way home. They got her into the house, and she seemed okay but then she collapsed again on 23 April on the way to the toilet. My sister called me and told me that Mom's eyes had turned white. At that moment I knew she was going to die. An hour later they rang to tell me she had gone. She was only 63, and she had so much potential that had never been realised. I think that had she been born in a different country, somewhere where she could have had a proper education, she might well have been a professional too.

I caught the night flight to Juba, accompanied by Motheo and Dr Charles Echelu, and cried uncontrollably on the plane.

My mother, Phoebe, and Dr Joseph Adrigwe on my wedding day

My mother had sacrificed so much to help me get an education in the early days, and the four years she managed to get me at St Joseph's had made possible everything that happened afterwards, but I hadn't been able to help her when she needed it most. She never gave up on me during the ten years I was gone from South Sudan, even when everyone else had. At one stage I locked myself in the aircraft toilet for privacy and wept for an hour, until someone knocked on the door to check that I was all right.

Because there was no proper mortuary in Juba, my mother's body was stored in a refrigerated container, piled up with dozens

211

of other bodies, wrapped only in a traditional African robe. I could never have imagined such an inhuman sight. I lifted the corner of the robe from her face; the skin was already laced with ice.

It was the first time that I really confronted the realisation that once you are dead, you are gone for good, and that when I died, I would be in exactly the same position. I felt angry and resentful and guilty, as well as frightened by the thought of my own mortality and the possibility that I might be taken before I had time to achieve everything I wanted to achieve.

I felt her death was my fault. I could have saved her if only I had persuaded her to leave South Sudan and live near me, but I know she would never have left the rest of her family and her church. Twelve of her grandchildren were living with her by the end and she would never have deserted them for the sake of her own health.

I felt the same way as her about the importance of maintaining family ties. Whenever I visited, I would always sleep in the family bed or on the floor, eating from the communal family plate. I would never think of going to a hotel. That had been one of the reasons for building her the house, in order for us all to be together in more comfort and to give the future children of the family a good start. In my mind I had always planned that once I could afford it, I would take off several months and spend time with her, making up for all the years that we had been apart, but it had all come too late. I had spent all my energy on trying to lift her and the rest of the family out of poverty, and I felt I had missed the opportunity to tell her how much I loved her.

The only coffin we could get was too small for her, and it was a struggle to get her arms into it in order to nail it shut. I had always wanted to buy a farm where she could be buried so that the children would know where she was and we would all have a permanent reminder of where we had come from. So for now we have sealed her in a concrete tomb so that we will be able to move her later if I can find the right place.

Around 1 500 people came to her funeral, which was held beside the house where I had hoped she would spend her old age, in a neighbour's mango plantation. The congregation included several government ministers who were either distant relatives or were people I knew. I bought three cows so that everyone would have enough to eat. She had risen in the administration of her church, and had delivered hundreds of babies as a midwife, and so was greatly respected by the community. Many of the people she had touched came to pay their respects. I felt very proud to be her son.

Again, I heard the words 'the will of God' coming from the lips of the priest during the service. I felt a stab of pain in my heart because I did not believe for a moment that my mother's early death was the will of God. We could not blame Him. He did not want my mother to die before her time. I believed that we were simply failing our own people, and our suffering was the result of our own weakness and laziness.

I mainly blamed the men, because I believe the purpose of all men in developing countries is to create security for the women. As men, we have none of the physical disturbances in our lives that women have to endure, and so we owe it to them to protect them as much as we can and give them opportunities in life. Many of the men who should be looking after the women and children of our family are either dead or failing to earn a living.

Most men in South Sudan only ever seem to destroy things and fight over stupid causes that mean nothing, and their women and children suffer the consequences. God did not give us muscles and intelligence in order for us to cause destruction. When I went to Uncle Martin's house during this visit, government soldiers shot a rival politician in a marketplace no more than 500 metres away, throwing his body into a car like an animal in full view of passers-by.

It is impossible for any honest person to prosper in such a system. Einstein said that the definition of insanity was to repeat the same mistakes over and over again and expect a different outcome, but in South Sudan, and in many other African countries, the same leaders and political parties keep coming back and doing the same things. This is why Africa remains a very poor continent despite all its abundant resources.

This trip was Motheo's first visit to South Sudan and the first time she met most of my extended family and the rest of her in-laws. She was warmly welcomed by all of them. When she wanted to help the women prepare food for the funeral guests, they shooed her away, telling her to relax and keep the older women company.

The conditions in Juba were an eye-opener for her: the guest-house we stayed at had a generator but it would only be on for a few hours each day and she had to use bottled water for everything, including brushing teeth. Then there were the potholed roads. She was also surprised by the many mud houses, and by the cattle, often emaciated, walking freely on the roads alongside motorists and pedestrians. However, most alarming was the presence all around the city of soldiers armed with AK-47s, many with a menacing look on their faces. Yet the locals seemed unfazed.

But I also tried to show her the beauty of my home country. I took her to the outskirts of the city where I was setting up my water bottling plant. The site was surrounded by open savannah and offered a view of the Nile River. She relished the rich mangoes that were in season at the time, and we enjoyed a delicious lunch at a restaurant overlooking the Nile.

Joseph's daughter, Emba, had been living with my mother and was now five years old. When I heard that her mother could not take her back because she had remarried, Motheo and I decided to adopt Emba. Her older brother stayed in South Sudan and I later paid for him to study in Uganda.

A few years later, when my medical practice was running smoothly, I was not only able to build a beautiful house for my family, but I also made proper provision for the education of our children. Moreover, I was able to assist 14 of my nephews and nieces to attend school and university. Sadly, due to the continuing fighting and chaos in South Sudan, the children all have to travel to other countries such as Uganda to continue their education, which makes everything far more expensive.

However, I was determined to help. I know that the only reason I have been able to achieve what I have is because of the generosity of people like the Comboni Missionaries and Franz Pahl, who made it possible for me to pursue my dreams. It is very common in Africa for one successful member of a family to support the children of others who are less fortunate. It is referred to as 'black tax', and I am very pleased to be in a position to be able to pay it.

Today, Motheo and I are the parents of four beautiful daughters, Naledi, Yeno and Awate, and our adopted daughter, Emba.

14 FAREWELL TO MY FATHER

Once my financial situation started to improve in early 2012, I went back to thinking about the water bottling project. By that time Thomas Greiten had moved on, married and taken another job in Germany, but I got back in contact with him. Despite all the physical and mental deprivations that he had endured in South Sudan, he did not like the idea that we had been defeated and he was as keen to try again as I was. Because Thomas wasn't free to drop everything and return to South Sudan himself, he recruited another guy, Marcel van Steen, who had previously been in the army, to build the factory structure.

Marcel arrived at the site in March 2012. It was a slow business because all the building materials had to come from Uganda, and it took us nine months to get the prefab structure up, put on the solar panels and do the drilling and testing. All the while Marcel suffered just as badly as Thomas had from the primitive living conditions. By December 2012 the structure was up, but then Marcel had to return to Germany for a short while. In the new year we had the electrical wiring done, put in the generator and did more water analysis.

I placed an order for a bottling machine, which would take a year to build. Our plan was to start production early in 2014, but in late 2013 fighting flared up once again after President Salva Kiir sacked his vice president, Riek Machar. This was after Machar publicly stated his intention to challenge Kiir for the presidency. The two men, who had belonged to the same political party before South Sudan gained its independence in 2011, went to war with each other, each recruiting their own fighters from tribesmen and creating fear and disruption among innocent citizens.

Yet again we had to put our project on hold. A temporary peace returned in August 2015 when a peace agreement was signed between the South Sudanese government and Machar's rebels. Marcel returned to South Sudan in 2016, and we were both optimistic that we would finally be able to get things off the ground.

However, just as we were about to start production at the plant, civil war resumed between the government forces and those of Machar. Marcel had to be evacuated by the German air force, leaving the new Sanaqua building standing empty and unproductive, another potent symbol of everything that has gone wrong in South Sudan over the last century.

When I first arrived in South Africa, I asked Father Enrico why the black population were so poor. I felt very upset by the injustices I could see all around.

'Why did God create us blacks poorer than the white people?' I asked.

'He didn't,' the Father replied. 'God created us in each image, irrespective of our colour, whether you are black, white or other races, with equal opportunities and abilities. However, our prosperity in life depends on your family circumstance, the economic situation of

During construction of our water bottling plant in Juba. Marcel van Steen is in the foreground in the top image.

The team involved in setting up the water bottling plant. Marcel van Steen is in the middle, with his father and another team member to his right. Thomas Greiten and Johnson Dudu Uni, a cousin of mine, are on Marcel's left.

Marcel with some of the building supplies for the plant bought in Uganda

your country and other things like bad leadership and circumstances.'

Now when I go back to South Sudan, I can see that God has been very fair because the people there have been given all the riches and resources of the world. We have fertile soil and oil and gold and enough water to make everything grow abundantly. God has more than fulfilled His side of the bargain.

South Sudan has been independent for many years but nothing is changing because we do not have the right people, with the right intentions, in the right places. This tragic situation has come about almost entirely because we have suffered from many decades of short-sighted and greedy leadership, leading to brutal and unnecessary civil wars and seemingly endless atrocities and acts of genocide. Nearly all of these were caused by the personal ambitions of the would-be leaders and by political misunderstandings that should have been resolved by talking and negotiating rather than killing, burning and raping.

Virtually all our recent politicians have fought and killed to become leaders because they lusted after power and money rather than for any altruistic reasons. Once they have gained those two things, nearly always by force, they do nothing but fight and instil fear in order to cling on to them. They have no plans to improve the lives of good, hard-working women like my mother, and instead of investing government money in developing the country they slide it into their own pockets and the pockets of those who stand close to them.

Power should not be an end in itself. Leaders should be able to support themselves on their legitimate salaries without plundering national resources that would be better spent building schools and hospitals and laying water pipes and electricity cables.

The leaders of South Sudan have nearly always come from poverty themselves, so of course they want to make themselves and their families secure before they worry about making life better for anyone else. But why is everyone in the country still so poor that anyone who gains a little power will do anything they can to get more money and security? Why is everyone corrupt and why does everyone have to be bribed to do anything?

I understand that corruption is a worldwide problem. Even in the West it is to be expected that if a metaphorical chicken lays ten eggs, six of them will be stolen, but that means there will still be four left with which to create more chickens. In many Asian countries it is more likely that nine of those eggs will disappear, but still the chicken population can survive. In Africa, however, not only do all the eggs disappear, but the chicken gets eaten as well.

Ordinary people are tired of the way politics are run, and they want to make changes. But they are even more worried about how they will be able to feed their families for another day, or where they will be able to get hold of medicine for a sick child. When you don't know where your next meal is coming from, it is impossible to focus on what should be done to improve things in the long term. It is too much to expect people to stand up for what is right if it means their families will be raped and murdered on the orders of those in power. And so they all accept their helplessness and concentrate on finding their next meal and nothing changes in the society.

Even now that I am an educated adult, I still don't understand how we have allowed this to happen. No matter how much time

I spend thinking, there are many things about my country and my people that don't make sense to me.

I have, for instance, taken many medical exams in Europe and I never score lower than the Europeans, always ending up among the top ten performers even though my education in South Sudan was interrupted for years at a time. So it isn't that the people of South Sudan are somehow less intelligent or less able than people from developed countries. So why, I ask myself, is there such a yawning gap between the medical care in Africa and in Europe if we are capable of producing equally high-performing doctors?

No matter how successful I might become in the world, I will always identify as South Sudanese. Sadly, being South Sudanese carries a stigma of being corruptible and of hopelessness. I firmly believe that I was not born in South Sudan by mistake; it's no coincidence that I was raised there. My journey was filled with setbacks and dangers. My determination and courage were tested over and over again. I could easily have given up at any one of the obstacles that were thrown up in my path, but I persevered.

I want the children of South Sudan to know that if they are willing to go out into the world in search of opportunities, and if they are willing to work hard, they can transform their lives and the lives of their families, and their country as a whole. There is no reason why South Sudan should not set out on a path to prosperity today, eventually taking its place among the richest nations in Africa.

In 2016, with all the work stress and worries about the bottling plant in South Sudan, I was again forgetting to eat or drink properly. Eventually my body rebelled, and my kidneys started to fail. I also developed irritable bowel syndrome and ulcers. I could tell that my body was not going to last long if I didn't change my ways.

At the same time, I wanted to start studying again and I realised I wouldn't be able to do that if I accidentally killed myself. I told Willem Schoonbee that I wanted to leave the hospital and return to studying.

'What do you want to study?' he asked.

'I want to do pulmonology,' I said. 'I see so many people in this area with lung problems because of the pollution. I want to be able to do as much for them as possible.'

'Okay,' he said, 'we'll give you a scholarship and pay you a salary while you study.'

I think I may well be the first black man to have been given such a generous offer from Mediclinic South Africa. I studied at Wits University, which was hard, but I was determined not to let Willem down. I was told that it takes most people three or four attempts before they pass their pulmonology exams. There are only about 90 pulmonologists in South Africa, only eight of them black, despite the fact that 80 per cent of the population is black. It was going to be a challenge to pass first time.

In the pulmonology department at Wits I was privileged to work with some of the best and most renowned academics in the field, professors whose knowledge and skills I had long admired. What struck me most, however, was that despite their stellar careers, they all still worked incredibly long days. I observed how they would often stay on campus after hours, and I realised that if they were willing to continue working so hard to learn and improve, then I could not rest or leave early if I hoped to gain even a fraction of their skills and knowledge. In order to maintain excellence in my career, I had to continue to strive for it.

I would drive the 130 kilometres from Trichardt to Johannesburg and back each day, and study hard in the evenings. I also continued seeing patients at the weekends to build on my practical experience, but I loved it. I didn't experience a single moment of racism during those two years. The group of candidates who sat the exams before me all failed. I became increasingly nervous as the moment of truth approached, and I was hugely relieved to hear I had passed the theory part.

During this time I tore my left thigh muscle, so I couldn't go to work. Sitting at home with my leg in a sling meant I was able to study even more. As a result of all this extra study time, I was the only one in my department to pass the oral exam, along with three others from Cape Town. I officially qualified as a pulmonologist in October 2018.

My friend David Zulu recently asked me why I did not go to church and respect Sundays as days of rest like he did. 'Do you think that because you are clever you are too good to thank God?' he asked.

'Listen,' I replied, 'we can agree that we are all made in the image of God, right? And the Bible tells us that God worked hard for six days to create the world and on the seventh day He rested. So we should also work hard, but if, by the end of the sixth day, we have still not succeeded in lifting everyone out of poverty, who are we to award ourselves a day off?'

In March 2019 I went on a two-week therapeutic bronchoscopy course, hosted by the University of Amsterdam in the Netherlands.

There I learned to use bronchoscopy (imaging the airways) to remove a foreign body, and also how to remove mucus plugs (a build-up of mucus) in the lungs using the same procedure. From Amsterdam I flew to the US for a conference on bronchoscopy. I couldn't have known it at the time, but this course and the conference would stand me in good stead just over a year later, when the COVID-19 pandemic swept the world.

In March I also opened my pulmonology practice at Midstream Mediclinic in Centurion.

I have travelled all over the world in order to broaden my knowledge and training and to increase my qualifications. I have now passed all the exams required to be a European Respiratory Society Diplomat. I think it would be reasonable to say that I am the most educated person of my generation to come out of the Equatoria region of Sudan, but however much I achieve, I don't think I will ever feel that I have done enough to deserve a rest. Hard work, I believe, is the only way for humankind to save itself. However much I achieve, it never feels enough.

Bishop Sandri remained a father figure and a friend to me throughout the years. He was always a phone call away if I needed any advice, whether relating to work, family or other problems. He agreed to be a trustee for a family trust I set up for my children. I bought him a new car and helped him with funds to support his passions for education and youth skills development. He loved South Africa so much, and he wished the government could start meaningful skills development to put right the injustices of the past. I would take him a panettone whenever we visited him in Witbank.

At the end of March 2019, shortly after I returned from my trip to the Netherlands and the US, he started to suffer from gastric pains, and then he collapsed. His GP had him admitted to hospital in Witbank, where I went to visit him. I was informed that the problem was just a peptic ulcer. At first I accepted this, but then, as I was driving home, I remembered what I had been told about my brother and mother just before they died. I immediately turned around.

By the time I got back to the hospital he had been admitted to the ICU, and they said he was confused. I was shocked to see how much he had deteriorated in such a short time; he was in septic shock with multi-organ failure. He was obviously dehydrated as a result of severe vomiting, but no one had fitted up a running fluid drip.

'Bishop,' I said, and he just rolled his eyes.

When the surgeon found out I was a pulmonologist, he suddenly sprang into action. It turned out that Bishop Sandri had a perforated ulcer and had been lying there for 12 hours with sepsis and multiple organ failure, including kidney failure. He was operated on at 11 pm that night, after resuscitation with fluid. Immediately after the operation he was put onto life support, a continuous dialysis machine and multiple drips to keep up his blood pressure. Ten days later he was taken off life support, but his body was swollen up with water because his kidneys were not working.

I spoke to the papal nuncio, the ambassador for the Vatican in South Africa, and asked if I could move him to Midstream Mediclinic. The nuncio agreed, since he knew I was like a son to Bishop Sandri and could be trusted to do my best on his behalf. Bishop Sandri was transferred the same day. We managed to drain 20 litres of water from his body, and he started walking around and eating.

About four days later, when I was doing my ward rounds, my hands started sweating and I suddenly felt an urge to go and visit him in the ICU. I found him totally lethargic, with low blood pressure. When I put a tube into his stomach he was bleeding ferociously. Because he presented late to the hospital in Witbank, and because they had left him so long before operating, they had been unable to control the ulcer effectively. I consulted one of the surgeons, who rushed him to theatre.

The operation was very difficult, and when he came back from theatre, he was on a ventilator for two days before he was taken off life support. Then he started to struggle to breathe, and I discovered that his right lung was filled with water. In pulmonology this is known as a whiteout: the fluid makes the lung appear white on an X-ray rather than the normal black. I asked a colleague to help me to put in a drain; I didn't think it would be good for me to do it because I was so close to him. Unfortunately, while performing the procedure, the Bishop's liver was punctured. He was then rushed back to theatre to control the bleeding and seemed to get better. A few days later, however, he started to bleed from a previous ulcer operation, and he was rushed to theatre again.

During his six weeks at Midstream the Bishop underwent several operations, but his condition didn't improve. Tragically, despite all our best efforts, Bishop Sandri passed away on 30 May 2019. The cause of his death was related to the bleeding ulcer, and I think even without the liver laceration his prognosis was not good.

I felt like I had lost my father. Just as with my mother, I had carried around so many plans in my head for the things I would

With Bishop Giuseppe (Joe) Sandri's family in Italy. His brother Fiorentino is on my left and Motheo, with Awate in front of her, is second from left.

do with him, and for him, now that I could afford to, in order to repay him a little for the kindness and support he had shown me throughout my life. But he was taken before I could put those plans into action. I was reminded again of how little time we all have and how important it is to do the things you want to do for those you love, and say the things you want to say, before it is too late and the opportunity has gone.

In December 2019 I took Motheo and the children to France and Italy. When we got to Rome, we visited Simon Donnelly, my old Afrikaans tutor and now a Vatican translator. Then we drove to the hills of Trentino in northern Italy to visit the village of Faedo, where Bishop Sandri came from. I met his brother, Fiorentino, who very kindly took time off to introduce me to the rest of the family, including his elderly sister, with whom the Bishop stayed when he returned to visit his family. They told me of how poor they had been during the Bishop's childhood and how much they had suffered in those days.

For the family, it had been very painful not to be able to travel to South Africa when Bishop Sandri fell ill and to assist him as they would have liked. To express their appreciation for my help, they organised a family celebration, with all the Bishop's sisters, brother, nieces and nephews, to officially introduce me and my family. 'We sadly lost a brother and uncle, but we found a new cousin and new family in South Africa!' Fiorentino said that day.

Later, one of the cousins showed me the family tree. My name had been added under that of Bishop Sandri as his son. I was deeply touched to think that he would have talked about me in such a fond way to his family.

15 ON THE FRONT LINE OF A PANDEMIC

I took Motheo and the children to Italy and France for Christmas 2019. Like the rest of the world, I was unaware that COVID-19, an infectious disease caused by the new coronavirus SARS-CoV-2, which was being recorded in Wuhan, China, had already reached Europe. I unwittingly brought my family into the path of the approaching storm. The more I read about COVID-19 upon our return, the more worried I became.

In January 2020 I developed flu-like symptoms, but they did not seem too worrying. I returned to work and people began to talk about whether we should be preparing for the virus to arrive in South Africa. The news from Italy, France and Spain was not good, and I was keen that we should learn from the experiences of these countries so that we would be ready to react more quickly. Since my area of specialisation is pulmonology, I was aware that if, or when, the virus did arrive, the sickest patients would be sent to me. I needed to build a team who could help me prepare the hospital to handle whatever was coming.

I was surprised by what happened next. Some doctors worried that if we concentrated too many of the hospital's resources on pre-paring to fight the virus, they would not be able to perform other operations, and that once the hospital was known to be a COVID-19 hospital, it would scare other patients away. Others feared that I was trying to turn the whole hospital over to dealing with a pandemic that they thought might not even reach us, and tried to get me removed from leadership of the COVID-19 response team.

I was convinced that it was right to prepare the hospital for a pandemic and, along with a physician, Dr Lee-Anne Godinho, I set about making all the necessary preparations. We did a great deal of research and wrote a protocol for the hospital on how to manage COVID-19 patients, ignoring the doctors who told us we were wasting our time.

For a while it looked as if the optimists would be be proved right and the virus might not reach us. Some patients, however, were already becoming nervous about coming into hospital for operations, causing the doctors to lose income, just as they feared they would. Some believed that Dr Godinho and I were deliberately spreading rumours that we were already treating COVID-19 patients, which was not true.

Still, the hospital's general manager was impressed by our protocol and I was asked to join the team of COVID-19 experts for Mediclinic International, which met once a week online, in order to learn from the experiences of doctors in other countries.

The outbreak then started to spread through the Muslim community of Laudium, in southwest Pretoria, and the waiting ICU beds were soon filled to capacity. Fearful that my predictions were now coming true and that other specialisations were about to be squeezed out by the emergency, one specialist colleague actually suggested to Dr Godinho that we should stop admitting patients from the Muslim community entirely, otherwise we would be over-whelmed and other doctors would not be able to earn a living.

There was no way I would turn patients away on that basis. Our first priority had to be to help the sick, not to protect our own incomes. Apart from anything else, it sounded like a dangerously racist idea. I never allow the idea of racism to cloud my judgement, because I do not believe I am less or more human than anybody else, hence I judge every situation according to its merits. We some-times blame our failure or our weakness on racism rather than tak-ing responsibility and facing the challenge. We then spend most of our energy and precious time entertaining the myopic thinking of a minority rather than really focusing on the issue of why we Africans are drowning in poverty while our so-called masters come and prosper in our own backyard.

Then the floodgates opened.

Many patients required mechanical ventilation and others suffered cardiorespiratory arrest even before being admitted to hospital. Our ICU filled up with patients being ventilated, with some having to lie on their stomachs for several hours to improve oxygen levels in their blood. I needed to work out a plan fast to assist these patients.

Soon I was working every waking hour. In the evenings I would call those who were infected to inquire how they were doing so that they would know they were not alone; we were in this together.

At the same time, fear of contracting the deadly virus was leading to increasing absenteeism among staff. Then two of our nurses became infected. Everybody was looking to me for guid-ance. I decided to hold a team-building and motivation session in the ICU over lunch, and laid out some takeaway chicken meals. We brainstormed about staff shortages, while listening to the nurses' concerns about personal protective equipment (PPE) and safety problems.

I was disappointed to discover that a member of staff had been deliberately throwing used needles and drips around, and taking pictures of these and sending them to the Department of Health, in the hope that the unit would be closed down as unsafe. This person felt that we did not have enough PPE and similar support to other private hospitals. One morning when I walked into the ICU, I was greeted by officials from the Department of Health, asking questions and making allegations that we were operating unsafely. Hospital management succeeded in convincing them that we would get on top of the problem.

In the following two months we treated nearly 300 patients and recorded 22 deaths, many of which were among elderly patients. The seriousness of the situation started to dawn and I was well aware that many of the people working on the wards were increasingly afraid of infection and needed to see that I was willing to accept the same level of risk as them. One day we had only half of the staff complement we needed because so many were quarantined, sick or exhausted. The senior nurses took responsibility, and each started to nurse three or four patients.

On the night of 20–21 June, after working on an emergency, I got home at four in the morning and slept until late that morning. When I woke, I was worried about the patient and decided to go back to the hospital in the afternoon. I was keen to have some company and asked Motheo, who also works at Midstream (at the time of writing she was graduating in cardiorespiratory physiotherapy) and had patients she could see, to come with me.

On the way, I overtook a truck, which I should not have done because it meant I crossed a solid line. My misdemeanour was witnessed by officers from the Tshwane Metro Police, who were parked by the side of the road in a 22-seater van and two unmarked sedans. They duly pulled me over.

One of the officers walked over to my side of the car, and I could see from his demeanour that he was angry. I rolled my window down and spoke to him in English. He replied in Sepedi, which I did not understand, so I asked him to speak in English.

'Step out of the car!' he demanded.

I got out and gave him my licence, noticing that his right hand was resting on his firearm, which was secured to his waist. I found this rather disconcerting. As he was not wearing a mask, I warned him that I was a doctor involved with the treatment of COVID-19 patients and that he should therefore keep a safe distance from me. For some reason this infuriated him even further.

I suspected that my being 'too black' and having a foreign accent, a South African wife and a nice German car were not working in my favour.

'You're under arrest for reckless driving and for overtaking on a solid white line,' he informed me.

I tried to reason with him, suggesting that it would be more appropriate to issue me with a ticket than to arrest me. I assumed that he would want a bribe, like so many other traffic officers who have stopped me, but he remained adamant that I was under arrest.

I asked if it was okay if Motheo got out of the car. He agreed, but as I moved away from him to tell her, he flew into a rage and started pushing me around.

'Why are you acting so aggressively?' Motheo asked him in English. She had gotten out of the car and was walking round to my side. 'Why are you treating him like a criminal? He isn't fighting with you.'

That infuriated the officer and he started shouting insults at her: 'You! You're a whore who sleeps with *makwerekwere*.'

I couldn't understand what he was saying because they were speaking in Sepedi, but I knew he had upset Motheo. She turned to me, saying that it would not be safe for her to leave me alone with him because she now feared for my life. Motheo is not someone who is overly dramatic, so I took her words seriously.

I took out my phone and started to record the encounter, asking Motheo to do the same. At that moment another male officer came over and, after a short discussion, we were instructed to get back into our vehicle and leave.

As we started to drive off, Motheo told me what the officer had been saying to her. I felt it was not acceptable to just drive away as if nothing had happened. I decided that I should record the registration number of the officers' vehicle. I stopped the car, but as I got out and started taking photos, two of them stormed at me. The next moment they had pressed me up against my car and handcuffed me roughly, with my hands behind my back.

The aggressive traffic officer rushed over to Motheo and tried to take her cellphone from her by force. He grabbed her by the neck, pushing her down towards the ground and dragging her to the van. She was screaming and trembling in fear, never having been mishandled this way.

When I was shuffled into the van seconds later, I could see that her lip was bleeding. When the officers weren't looking, I slipped my phone over to her and told her to send the videos I had recorded to a friend of mine, but at that moment she was too traumatised to hear me. By then the officers, who had gotten hold of her phone, had deleted the videos and photos on her device, which didn't have a password.

The aggressive officer demanded my phone and got into the vehicle. I told him I had left it in my car, but he insisted that he had seen me carrying it and searched me. It was during this search that he looked straight into my eyes: 'I will kill you like George Floyd!' Then he grabbed me by the throat in front of his colleagues and started choking me.

I believe I may have lost consciousness as I struggled to breathe, but I can remember hearing Motheo screaming. When she saw my eyes rolling back into my head, she handed over my phone and the policeman ordered me to give him the PIN to unlock it. At this stage I was struggling to comprehend what I had been told to do and when I didn't obey him instantly he again grabbed me by the throat.

All the while two of his female colleagues stood idly by and watched the attack from outside the van. Motheo heard one of them saying, 'We have to take crap from white people but we're not going to take crap from black people.'

I realised at that moment how easy it would be for him to kill me. The chances were that his colleagues would cover up for him if that happened, making up a story that would make it sound like self-defence. And if I died, what would happen to Motheo and the kids? I was terrified, and kicked out in an attempt to free myself, but without success. One of his colleagues then grabbed him and he released his grip.

I finally realised that I had been told to unlock my phone and obeyed. After I had done so, he deleted the videos and photos that I had taken, even going as far as logging into my Facebook account and inspecting my other social media apps to ensure that I had not posted the incident on any of them. After he was satisfied that everything had been deleted, he told us that we were both under arrest.

On the way to the Lyttelton police station in Centurion, the police officer was seated next to me and had a video call with his daughter, laughing and talking as if nothing unusual had happened, as if he hadn't just attacked the father of girls just like his own. When we arrived at the station, I was handcuffed to a safe next to one of the desks. They charged me and Motheo with reckless and negligent driving, criminal injury and assault.

If this police officer had been white, the incident would have brought protesters to the streets. But because he is black, people express their disapproval and seem to expect no better. I firmly believe that we can do better. As Africans, we need to first liberate ourselves from the mentality of victimhood and self-entitlement. I believe this is the reason why we remain stuck in the past and are so quick to blame our former colonial masters for what happens in our lives. By doing so, we accept that they are superior to us and that they can control our minds and hence our failures. I refuse to submit to this way of thinking.

I called Dr Shane Kotzé, the hospital manager at Midstream

Mediclinic, who arranged for a lawyer to come to the station and get us out on bail. We were detained for approximately four hours, and all that time I was handcuffed. Needless to say, it was incredibly humiliating, and it brought back memories of all the times I was unjustly arrested or robbed during my journey from South Sudan. But this time there was a difference because I was no longer alone. Not only was Motheo by my side throughout the ordeal, but I now also had a great many people who I could reach out to for support. I was no longer some homeless, penniless child.

I had people who would speak up on my behalf, to the media and to the Metro Police, and in the following days that was what they all did. The media coverage was overwhelmingly sympathetic.

After the media reports, Motheo was contacted by the Independent Police Investigative Directorate (IPID) and she laid an official complaint on our behalf. We also instituted a civil case, because we felt that if there were no repercussions for these officers, they would simply continue with their actions against civilians. At the time of writing, the case was still pending.

Motheo was so traumatised by the incident that she went for therapy. She had never before witnessed such violence or been physically manhandled like that.

All my life I have refused to be a victim. No matter what obstacles have been thrown at me, I have always remained positive and optimistic about the future. Neither racism nor xenophobia will cause me to change that view.

One day early in July I was called to an emergency. One of my junior doctors needed help with performing an intubation to get a patient onto life support. In my rush to prevent the patient from dying, I forgot to put my protective goggles on. A week later I was struck down by a blinding headache, something I had never experienced before. My eyes were intensely painful and my whole body felt freezing cold. At first I thought it might simply be exhaustion catching up with me, as I was working 15 or 16 hours a day and living on coffee at the time.

When I did a COVID-19 test, the result was negative. This was at a time when the pandemic was at the peak of its first wave in South Africa, and I was sure that if I allowed myself to fall ill my team would collapse under the pressure. During the days I took paracetamol to keep me functioning, despite suffering shortness of breath. But the nights were terrible, leaving me drenched in sweat.

While on an ICU round, I suffered a fainting episode. I was hypertensive, with a slow heart rate. I had lost two patients due to cardiac arrest, and the majority of COVID-19 patients on ventilators were hypertensive, some with a slow heart rate. At this point I feared for my own life. I lost five kilograms in five days, which I put down to the sweating.

Still I tested negative for COVID-19, but when I went for a CT scan of my lungs, what I saw was 100 per cent in line with COVID-19. I took some steroids and blood thinners and tried to get more sleep. Thankfully, I soon started to feel better.

A few weeks later I did an antibody test, which confirmed that I indeed had had COVID-19.

Ever since the pandemic broke out, doctors and scientists all over the world have been working hard to discover new ways to prevent and treat COVID-19 symptoms, and to save lives. In early 2020, during the first few months of the pandemic, I was as intrigued as anyone. It felt like I was being offered a completely new set of challenges, and a chance to make a contribution to the health of the world.

As a pulmonologist, I was particularly focused on the needs of patients with breathing difficulties that lead to abnormally low concentrations of oxygen in their blood, a condition known as hypoxaemia. Towards the end of June, some of my patients were dying after seven days on life support, which I didn't think was acceptable.

Everything I had read suggested to me that COVID-19 patients die because of lung fibrosis or thrombosis. I started to question why they were developing fibrosis so soon, as fibrosis usually develops only after several weeks. I also couldn't understand why they were dying from blood clots when they were on blood thinners, with high to normal blood pressure.

A doctor in his seventies was in our ICU with severe COVID-19. He had been on life support for more than a week when he started to deteriorate. I decided to investigate what was happening in his lungs and did a bronchoscopy. This procedure involves passing a thin imaging tube, or bronchoscope, through a patient's nose or mouth, down the throat and into the lungs. A tiny fibre-optic camera attached to the tip of the tube allows the doctor to see what is going on in the airway in real time.

As far as I know, this was the first-ever bronchoscopy performed on a patient who had been on life support for more than a week. As I watched the image on the monitor, I saw something moving up and down the airway as the patient breathed. Initially I thought it was a tumour. But when I tried to grab it with the endoscopic forceps, it started to stretch. That was when I realised it was a mucus plug.

Up to this point, the COVID-19 literature had said people who have the virus don't develop mucus, so no one had thought to look for it. Furthermore, the mucus was usually deep down in the airways and had often started to harden. We discovered that COVID-19 patients can indeed develop mucus, and that it was the mucus that was blocking the small airways. This is why giving these patients more and more oxygen wasn't helping: they weren't dying of lung fibrosis or thrombosis, but from mucus plugs.

When a patient on life support can't take up all the oxygen they are given, the ventilator alarm goes off to indicate that the pressure in the lungs is becoming too high. Previously, we thought this was an indication that the patient had entered the final phase of the disease, referred to as Type H COVID-19 pneumonia, and we would have to accept that the patient was dying.

However, that day we managed to remove the mucus plugs from the lungs during a procedure that lasted two hours. We were exhausted afterwards, but it was worth it as the patient could be taken off life support the next day. In the following weeks I went on to do more than 60 bronchoscopies to remove mucus plugs; 85 per cent of the patients who would previously have been considered terminal survived.

The use of bronchoscopies in the fight against COVID-19 had been neglected for fear of spreading the infection. If it is not done in the right setting, it does pose a significant risk for both the patient and the doctor, who is exposed to infection during the procedure.

However, I now had proof that when it is done in a correct setting, it will save lives.

Soon post-mortem studies were published in support of my findings, and in October 2020 I published an article on my findings with Professor Guy Richards in the *African Journal of Thoracic and Critical Care Medicine*. Many doctors are fearful of being infected during the procedures, but I feel it is not the time for us to down tools out of fear for our own lives. A doctor takes an oath to serve.

I should mention that the World Health Organization initially discouraged the use of bronchoscopy in COVID-19 patients owing to the risk of spreading the infection. In November 2020, the South African Department of Health also circulated a memo in which it addressed the matter of therapeutic bronchoscopy for mucus removal in patients with COVID-19. According to the memo, this treatment was considered a high-risk procedure and 'extreme caution' was advised when it is used as an intervention in COVID-19 patients; its routine use for the removal of mucus is not recommended at present. However, the memo also stated that it may be considered as an intervention 'to be performed only under strict conditions by experienced staff to minimise risks'.

As we learned more about the disease, guidelines changed, and published studies now show that bronchoscopy can be a safe treatment option. I believe this shows again how we, as doctors, are in a position to explore interventions to improve the care of our patients, if approached in a responsible way. While not all hypoxaemic COVID-19 patients get mucus plugs, some do and the fact remains that we have been able to save the lives of many COVID-19 patients by removing mucus plugs.

The second wave of COVID-19 that hit South Africa in December 2020 was just as cruel as the first. It was one of the most depressing periods in my life, knowing that we did not have enough intensive care resources to save everybody – not even those who could afford to pay. No matter how rich or poor, white or black a patient was, they all needed the same beds. The decisions as to who should get life support and who should not, were down to me. But my passion and my calling, to help all the sick who came to me, made it impossible for me to choose. I believed everyone deserved a chance, irrespective of their age or co-morbidities, but the reality was that we did not have enough resources for everyone. Time was critical and every second someone somewhere was losing his or her life because of a lack of oxygen. Something, which is normally free to all of us from the air we breathe, had become a rare commodity. One day, I thought, this will be me and somebody else will be deciding if I deserve to live or die. The unfairness of it all was difficult to comprehend, but it made me even more determined to help as many people as possible.

The pandemic continued and in July 2021 the third wave hit South Africa. Once again, I was struck by the fear that COVID-19 caused. Fear of losing a loved one, fear of not being able to breathe, fear of dying. And fear makes people irrational.

During this time our patients were mostly white people, in contrast to the patient profile during the first wave, when almost all our patients were from the Indian community in Laudium. Many of the patients presented with liver disease, which was disconcerting, especially among younger people. It intrigued me, because although there had been reports of liver disease in COVID-19 patients before, this was usually seen in obese or severely over-weight cases, not fairly young and otherwise seemingly healthy people.

We realised that many of the patients presenting with liver disease had been taking ivermectin, an antiparasitic drug commonly used in veterinary medicine and only in very specific cases and small doses to treat parasitic infections in human patients. Claims that ivermectin was an effective treatment against COVID-19 were rife, even though there was no conclusive large-scale clinical evidence of this, and health authorities across the world had cautioned against its use, especially in large doses. In fact, the US Food and Drug Administration later specifically advised against the use of ivermectin.

People were taking whatever form of ivermectin they could find, usually the veterinary version and at unregulated doses – too much for human use – grasping at a 'miracle drug'. The problem, though, is that ivermectin dampens the symptoms of COVID-19, which makes people think that it is working. But because it does not kill the virus, the patient becomes sicker and sicker, and by the time they get to the hospital it is almost too late, because by then their oxygen levels are generally very low. They struggle to breathe and their liver function is already compromised.

I realised again how profoundly fear can affect our decision-making powers. It overrides our ability to think rationally and makes us susceptible to misinformation. I even saw patients in hospital taking ivermectin. What struck me was that many of the patients embracing this so-called treatment, for which there was no scientific evidence, came from deeply religious backgrounds. It made me recall how I too grew up in a community where faith was accepted as the solution to all problems.

When I was growing up, we simply assumed that when bad things happened, it was God's will. We learned to accept things we shouldn't have accepted. We accepted that it is normal not to have a proper toilet. We accepted that it is normal to eat on the floor. We accepted that it is normal to live in dirty conditions. We prayed and prayed, but nothing changed. We simply suffered more.

If our lives turn out the way they do simply because it is God's will, then God must surely be racist. Why else would things be so bad in Africa while going well in Europe and America? The problem with accepting a poor outcome as God's will, when in fact it is the result of people's bad decisions, is that it absolves us of responsibility. It validates the person who made the decision as a hero because they are 'doing God's will', and it makes us powerless to help ourselves. If we believe that bad things are God's will, how can they change? How can things improve if we don't take responsibility for our own actions and decisions?

Accepting bad things as God's will is a misrepresentation of God, I think. Our relationship with God is a deeply personal one. But the decisions we make every day have got nothing to do with Him; decisions are made by humans. God works through our brains, our abilities to reason and be creative. When we start thinking about a problem and take steps to solve it, things get moving. Only then will things begin to change.

In my view, this is where we often get it wrong in Africa. We have never accepted that the decisions we made in the past are at the heart of our problems; we would rather point a finger at someone else and blame them for our hardship. And by never owning our decisions, we also never move forward, because we believe that changing our circumstances is not within our power.

The COVID-19 pandemic has exposed many of Africa's weaknesses. But it has also shown us how much potential we have. We have abundant resources, a youthful population, intelligent people. Africa is a sleeping giant. But the continent's potential cannot be realised if we don't take responsibility for our own fate. Maybe the solutions to Africa's problems start with separating them from God. The hardship we see in Africa is not because of God's will; it is because of us, what we do – or don't do. The solutions, and the action, must come from us.

16 THE SECOND HALF

In Africa we tend to forget about planning for the future, focusing instead on the here and now, just to survive. But I have learned that living is about more than just surviving.

I think of my life as being divided into two halves. From birth to the age of 45 is the first half; the time after 45 is the second half. Think of what happens during a football match. Before the match starts, there's a warm-up. To me, that's the period from birth to when you're about 25 years old. It's the time when I learned about life, got an education and prepared for adulthood.

Then, at the age of 25, my first half started. In the first half of a football game, the players are fresh, they have lots of energy and they are eager to score goals. The game is fast. But the first half is also the time when the team make mistakes, because they're keen for a win. It was also like that for me. I set my goals: I wanted to get married, raise a family, have a house and be the best I could be in my career. People thought I was crazy going about life like that, being so focused on achieving my goals. But because I had this thinking, things have fallen into place, and I have achieved these goals.

I will turn 45 in September 2022. It will be the start of my second half. In the second half of a football game, play is more considered, perhaps slower, because it is the time to consolidate the mistakes of the first half and think more strategically about winning. This is where I am now; I'm no longer in survival mode. I'm not hungry any more, I have a house, my children's education is paid for and I've become an expert in my career.

My second half will be the most important part of my life and my goal is to leave the world in a better state than I found it. Because I'm now in a better position personally, I can look beyond myself and focus on others, and have a better perspective on how to effect change. It is like being at the top of a mountain, from where you are able to see a bigger, clearer view of a problem.

Why do Africans lack leadership skills? Why is Africa so far behind the rest of the world? Why are we so good at following other people's instructions, but so bad at seeing what needs to be done and doing it for ourselves?

It's not that we lack the necessary intellect – because many Africans win places at the best universities in the world, from Harvard to Oxford. It's also not that we don't have the practical skills – because when foreign companies come to Africa, we are perfectly capable of carrying out their instructions and creating great things. But the moment the foreigners return home, nothing else happens and everything that has been created starts to deteriorate. Singapore gained its independence at the same time as many African countries, but just look at how the Singaporeans have been able to build on what they were left with. Look what the Chinese are able to achieve when they come to Africa to build roads and other infrastructure.

Yet so often bright young Africans who have travelled or studied abroad fail to channel their academic achievement into improving the situation in their own countries. When they return home, they become so focused on making money and achieving status for themselves that they are unable to see how to improve their countries, or even maintain them. They would rather spend their money on expensive cars and champagne than invest it in brick factories, building roads or the infrastructure needed to give homes running water and toilets. Even though they have seen how much better people's lives are in Europe, America and the Far East, they do not seem to have the will, the imagination or the application to do the same for their own people.

These are the people who will be our leaders in a few years' time – and who have the power to either break or perpetuate the cycle of hopelessness. The answer lies in education, and how we teach our children. We not only have to give our children the necessary knowledge and skills but also build curiosity, self-confidence, tenacity and perseverance to help them effect the changes needed at a practical level.

That is why, in my second half, I want to focus on building schools in Africa, starting in South Sudan and then South Africa. But these schools have to be right for Africa and have to equip children with the appropriate knowledge, skills and attitude.

Africa has huge potential, but that potential is not realised when you don't have the skills needed to fix problems. The solutions need not be grand schemes; we simply need to start with getting the basics right – good nutrition, good sanitation, good education, good family structures.

South Sudan has been at war for a long time, and it is the children who have suffered the most. The war has created generations of disadvantage. Having children of warring tribes in the same schools can go a long way to breaking down divides. But it's not enough just to have them learn together in the same school; I want them to work together to build those schools. Because after a year of working together to build something, will you still fight each other? I don't think so. Because working together on building something breaks down any assumptions we have of one another. And wars are nearly always fought over assumptions.

I know my plans are ambitious. It will take a lot of money to get this project off the ground. But I have learned along my journey that you don't have to have the complete solution in place in order to fix a problem. You simply have to start somewhere, and keep moving. I don't have all the money yet to build a school, but I do have enough to start drawing up plans, and that's what we've done. By working at a problem in small steps, you keep moving forward and things gradually fall into place.

When people see that things are happening, they want to be part of the change. I was amazed how, after just one presentation to a group in Cape Town, people came up to me to offer their help and put me in touch with others who can contribute their expertise in areas that I don't know anything about. That is the beauty of opening your mind and taking small steps towards creating change. People notice you, without your having sought their attention.

When you think of positive things, they start to happen. It is like when I was walking through the forest as a boy, with absolutely no possessions or money. Most of the time I was not thinking about wild animals, or criminals or people who might attack me. I was just walking. I was happy, because I was moving forward. And nothing bad happened. Anything you put your mind to is possible, if you take those first steps, work hard at it and keep thinking positively.

At 65, when I reach the end of my second half, maybe I'll hang up my boots. Then I will go into extra time. I would love to be a role model for others by then, knowing that the things I did in my first and second halves have helped to make the world a better place, and maybe I can inspire others to live a second half that will leave a positive legacy, too.

Part of being successful, I think, is finding solutions to obstacles along the way. People often say that we learn from our failures. But I don't agree: if we had learned from our failures, Africa would surely be the most developed continent in the world – because we have failed repeatedly at absolutely everything!

In my view, we learn from our mistakes, not our failures. When we fail, it means we don't try again, and then we've learned nothing. But when we make mistakes and try a different way the next time, that's when we learn. It is the times when things do not seem clear, and when we have to work at trying to understand them, that make us who we are.

I made a mistake when I went to Kenya the first time, trying to get across the border on my own rather than taking the bus. My attempt went horribly wrong. But I didn't give up; instead, I went back to point A and started again, trying a different way. I didn't fail in my mission; I simply made a mistake in how I approached it.

Correcting a mistake and trying again is hard work, and it calls for a lot of determination. It is often not comfortable, and it is always easier to ignore the problem in the hope that it will simply go away. Yet if we don't address a problem in a timely fashion, it can become a crisis. When we look back on a crisis, we often see that the underlying problem has existed for a long time but people chose to ignore it, because it seemed easier that way.

I see this in the hospital, too. The second wave of the COVID-19 pandemic hit South Africa in December 2020, at a time when people usually take their summer holidays. We didn't have enough nursing staff in the intensive care unit, yet we had to handle more patients than before. We learned from this experience, and when the third wave hit (in July 2021), we were prepared to handle far more patients than in either of the two previous waves – and we recorded the least number of deaths. That was a big reward. But it would not have been possible if we had not learned from our previous experiences.

Late in 2021, I was nominated for the 2022 Aurora Prize for Awakening Humanity, which is awarded every year by the Aurora Humanitarian Initiative in recognition of individual efforts to address humanitarian challenges. (At the time of publication, the winner had not yet been announced.) It came as a complete surprise. It is not something you can apply for; in fact, I did not even know I was in the running!

The same thing happened when I was announced as the *Daily Maverick*'s 'African Person of the Year' in 2021, and named as one of the 100 most influential Africans by *New African* magazine in 2020. I could never have imagined in my wildest dreams that such honours would come to me. I embarked on my journey not to be noticed by people but simply because I was determined to make a better life. I have endured many hardships along the way, but I know today that it has all been worth it.

Life's journeys are not equal; some are easier than others. But those that start from an uncomfortable departure point often bring the greatest reward, simply because you have more motivation to move forward. You have very little to lose when there are no comfortable surroundings to fall back on.

Every difficult situation is an opportunity to learn and grow – and that is a choice. How we respond to obstacles along our way is entirely up to us. We can choose to be victims of the circumstances and simply accept the outcome or learn from hardship and take responsibility for our decisions and actions, even when things look particularly bleak. My experiences of being betrayed and dismissed by people who were supposed to support me – missionaries in Eritrea, James, my partner on the streets of Asmara, my relatives in Kenya – were extremely disheartening. But giving up was not an option, and had I not chosen to keep going, I would not have got to where I am today.

My journey has also taught me that good education is fundamental to breaking the cycle of helplessness and poverty we see in Africa, and I'm honoured to be an ambassador for the Rally to Read programme, an initiative to give children and teachers in rural schools access to quality learning materials. Only if we allow our children to learn, and equip them with the right skills, will they become agents of change.

But children do not learn only from books; they also learn from role models. That's why my involvement in educational initiatives such as Rally to Read, and as an ambassador for the Ruth First Jeppe Memorial Trust, is such an honour – because it is an opportunity for me to help shape a generation's future.

I am very proud to have been recognised at this level, especially when it has come so unexpectedly. When I heard that I'd been named African Person of the Year, I was deeply humbled. It was proof to me that the ability to excel is not determined by colour, personality, age, religion or gender. What makes one excellent is the ability to not give up.

These awards do not change who I am or how I go about life. In fact, what they have done is to rekindle the flame in me to achieve yet more. The awards do not mean that I have arrived, but show that my journey is not yet complete.

I am no longer an anonymous boy. The world is noticing me – Africa is noticing me – and I need to move forward and make something out of this gift. It brings a lot of responsibility but also an opportunity to be a role model and achieve the goals I have set out for my second half. My journey, and the lessons I've learned along the way, have shown me that I can close my first half with a big smile and stride into my second half with confidence.

ACKNOWLEDGEMENTS

As you would have seen from reading this story, I owe many people my gratitude for believing in me and supporting me through my life. Above all, however, I would like to thank Motheo, my wife. It is not easy to live with someone who is as driven as I am, and she has never wavered in her love and support. On top of everything that I have loaded onto her shoulders, she has also found the time to be a wonderful mother and physiotherapist. My love and admiration for her are boundless.

This book would not have been possible without the brilliant Andrew Crofts and his wife, Susanne. Thank you for welcoming me into your home and making me feel comfortable. I appreciate every effort you made, and you have truly understood me well.

I would also like to thank my personal assistant, Bruna dos Santos, who joined my practice in 2014. She not only helps to ensure the financial health of my practice but also has taken over the running of a great part of my life. She is not only a friend, she is like a mother to me. Bruna, her husband Toni, and daughters Marzia, Gianna and Adriana make me feel like part of their family.

To my in-laws, especially my mother-in-law, Elizabeth Phalatse: thank you for welcoming me so warmly into the family and for

THE BOY WHO NEVER GAVE UP

your support and assistance with our young children. You are a loving grandmother to them and a pillar of strength to us all.

To my uncles, Alex, Martin and Victor: thank you for your role in my upbringing. To my sisters Sarah Tereka, Agnes Meling and Diana Nyoka: we have been through a lot of hardship, in particular the loss of our beloved mother, but we have stood strong as a family. Sarah, thank you for stepping in after our mother passed on, and for supporting and managing the family.

I was rejected by my family many times, but at the same time I have been accepted by my new family. I would like to thank my family in Italy: my uncle, Fiorentino Sandri, and his children, Federico, Fiamma and Elisa, and my aunts, Gigliola, Maria and Berta – thank you all for your support and love.

My thanks to Gottfried Pessl, Eleonora Pessl and Stefan Pessl for welcoming us to your home in Graz and for your support during my journey.

To my brothers Thomas Greiten and Marcel van Steen: I am lucky to have you in my life, and I know deep inside that we will complete the project once things settle down. I thank Marcel's dad for coming to South Sudan to help with the building of the warehouse. David, thank you for your support and for visiting South Sudan during the construction.

My thanks to Hanlie Retief, for her encouragement in getting my story published, and for introducing me to Annie Olivier of Jonathan Ball Publishers. You are truly angels sent to smooth the path of my journey.

To my best friend, Rodney Mudau, and his wife, Motsoka Mudau, thank you for naming your son after me. We have come a long way together. Though we may sometimes go for long periods without seeing each other, ours is a friendship that has endured simply because of an unseen and unspoken bond of brotherhood.

To my good friend Salome Dlangamandla and her husband, Tshepo Mokoka, thank you very much for being part of my family. When we met in 1999 you said I would be great one day, but it is only because of the support of people like you.

To my good friends Dr Neo Rakumakoe and his wife, Serwalo, and Dr Thabo Mokotong and his wife, Rose-D, and my godson Khumo, I still remember those crazy days at Steve Biko Academic Hospital, the registrar politics and that memorable trip to the USA.

Thanks to the Comboni Missionaries for their support during my journey and for believing in me. And special thanks to Brother Peter Niederbrunner and family, including his nephew Markus. Without Brother Peter's support, I would not be here today, and he has had a pivotal role in my life.

I would like to thank everyone at Mediclinic Highveld for putting up with me during those difficult early days. Thanks to Willem Schoonbee and his wife for always being there for me and for assuring me that things would be okay, and to my nursing team on Ward G, especially Sisters Sonet Goosen and Felicia Buthelezi, but not forgetting all the other nurses and colleagues who contributed to the management of my patients.

At Mediclinic Midstream – my new family – special thanks to Dr Shane Kotzé and the team, in particular for enabling me to participate in the COVID-19 expert forum, from which I have learned so much. Thanks also to the A-team in the Critical Care

Unit: without this dedicated group of professional nurses, Mediclinic Midstream would not have been able to lead in the fight against COVID-19. To my colleagues, Dr Lee-Anne Godinho and Dr Cornel Engelbrecht, thank you for your unwavering support in the fight against COVID-19: we stand tall because of teamwork.

Thanks to my practice partner, Dr Kelebogile Khomo, who held the fort while I was doing my fellowship in pulmonology. Your passion, determination and consistency are admirable.

Thank you to all those who guided and mentored me during my time as a fellow and as a pulmonologist, especially Emeritus Professor Guy Richards, Professor Ismail Kalla, Professor Rajen Morar and Emeritus Professor Charles Feldman. Thanks also to Professor Michelle Wong, for believing in me, and to Professor James Ker and Professor Greg Tintinger of the University of Pretoria, for laying the foundation of my career.